The Journey of the "I" into Life

The Journey of the "I" into Life

A FINAL DESTINATION OR A PATH TOWARD FREEDOM?

Lectures from the 2012 International
Waldorf Early Childhood Conference
at the Goetheanum in Dornach, Switzerland

The Journey of the "I" into Life: A Final Destination or a Path Toward Freedom?
First English Edition
© 2012 Waldorf Early Childhood Association of North America

ISBN: 978-1-936849-18-5

English Edition Editor: Nancy Blanning
Managing Editor and Graphic Design: Lory Widmer
Front cover illustration (from the conference program) by Olaf Auer. Taken from the stage scenery "Cosmic Memories" for the eurythmy performance 29.720 – *Ich* of Vera Koppehel. Lighting by Marc Bott, photography by Charlotte Fischer, design by Philipp Tok.
Back cover photo: Conference participants at the Goetheanum. Photo courtesy of Janni Nichol.

This publication was made possible by a grant from the Waldorf Curriculum Fund and produced in cooperation with the International Association for Steiner/Waldorf Early Childhood Education (IASWECE).

Waldorf Early Childhood Association of North America
285 Hungry Hollow Rd.
Spring Valley, NY 10977
845-352-1690
info@waldorfearlychildhood.org
www.waldorfearlychildhood.org

For a complete book catalog, contact WECAN or visit our online store: store.waldorfearlychildhood.org

All rights reserved. No part of this book may be reproduced in any form without the written permission of the publisher, except for brief quotations embodied in critical reviews and articles.

A Note on the Text

Because no full recording or transcription was made of these lectures, the content of this book was gathered in several different ways.

In general, Nancy Blanning's notes, taken in English, served as the basis of the written version. Louise deForest and Renate Long-Breipohl reviewed these notes and added their own revisions and clarifications. Edmond Schoorel provided his written notes to be compared and combined with Nancy's version, and approved the final result.

Two lectures were given in German, with a simultaneous English translation that formed the basis of the notes. Michaela Glöckler reviewed and revised these, as well as adding selected images from her presentation. Claus-Peter Röh supplied his German notes, which were translated with the help of Michael Widmer and combined with the English version.

Thus, these written "lectures" are not simply a record of what was heard at the conference, but in many cases supplement or clarify what took place there. The lectures have been thoroughly reviewed and revised by the authors to ensure that the thoughts each one wished to convey are accurately represented, which in some cases meant adding material that was not part of the spoken presentation.

We hope that for those who attended the conference, these lectures will be a valuable extension of what was experienced there; and for those who did not, they can be studied independently for their rich treasures of pedagogical wisdom.

Contents

Preface ~ 9

Our Children:
Our Guides Toward Becoming Truly Human ~ 11
Louise deForest, USA
Sunday, April 1, 2012

From Unbornness to I-consciousness:
The Three Great Steps of Incarnation ~ 21
Dr. Michaela Glöckler, Switzerland
Monday, April 2, 2012

The I, the Self, and the Body:
Steps Going Up and Steps Going Down ~ 33
Dr. Edmond Schoorel, Netherlands
Tuesday, April 3, 2012

Working with Accelerated and Delayed
Development in Early Childhood Education ~ 45
Dr. Renate Long-Breipohl, Australia
Wednesday, April 4, 2012

Twelve Doorways to the World:
The I and the Body in Sensory Existence ~ 65
Claus-Peter Röh, Switzerland
Thursday, April 5, 2012

Biographical Notes ~ 77

Preface

Rudolf Steiner's art of education was meant to serve the whole world, not just a single continent or country. What is universal in this education is that an I or a person or a Self wants to identify itself with an inherited body. Only with reverence can we meet this fact. How this I finds its way to the available body, finds a relationship to it, a feeling of being at home in it, depends in great measure on education. Among other important factors in the first seven years of life—such as nutrition, sensory experience and rhythm—Rudolf Steiner adds the capacity for imitation, which plays an important role in supporting the individuality in gradually taking hold of the physical body as its instrument and fully developing its creativity.

During the 2012 World Early Childhood Conference our hope was to explore such questions as the following: How must our activity as educators be so that it can be imitated and can stimulate free creative play? How can our storytelling stimulate powers of imitation more intensively? How can our rhythmic games and finger plays be prepared and structured so that the children can participate in them more actively? What therapeutic/educational supports can we develop for children who are either hyperactive or apathetic? What practical consequences can we draw from Rudolf Steiner's teachings about the twelve senses?

Over a thousand people from 54 countries attended the conference. For those who were not able to attend, as well as those who were present, we are pleased to be able to offer these lectures as an aid to further work on the conference theme.

—Adapted from the conference program

Our Children:
Our Guides Toward Becoming Truly Human

∼ **Louise deForest, USA**

It is quite impressive to see all of you, considering the long distances you have traveled. Welcome to you all!

I want to start by telling you about my first experience in the classroom. I never wanted to be a teacher; at three years old, when asked what I wanted to be, I said I wanted to be a work horse—one of those beautiful Belgian work horses. I preferred almost any profession over being a teacher, but the doors to other possibilities kept closing. So in my mid-twenties I gave in and decided to be a teacher. I started my teaching career in a daycare center, working with young three-year-old children. That is where I met Natasha. She was the only child of a poor, uneducated family. Her skin was pasty white—a sure sign of lack of nutritious food—she was obese and had a little upturned nose. She had tiny blue eyes and long, straggly hair. Every day she would stand in the door with her large body and announce, "I'm here," in a whiney, nasal voice. Outwardly I treated Natasha fairly, just as every other child; whenever she wanted, she sat on my lap and she joined in all our activities. She was a member of the group, but inwardly it was clear to me that I did not like her. When she would announce her presence, I would experience a sinking feeling in myself and would inwardly groan. I was glad to see Natasha move on to the four-year-old class.

But I have never forgotten Natasha; all these years later she is still with me. I failed Natasha. Natasha invited me to go on a journey with her, which I refused to take. She was providing me with an opportunity to develop and learn something that I had not yet learned. I think Natasha sacrificed herself for my growth as a teacher and now I always feel her right behind me.

Every child comes into life with an intention, choosing a country, language, culture and family. There is great wisdom guiding these choices. Every child has an intention in coming to us in the classroom, as well. Each child comes to receive gifts from us that perhaps we do not even know we have—aspects of ourselves that they can use in their life to come. They also come to strengthen us in areas which we have not yet developed or where we are weak, to help overcome something within ourselves that we may also not be aware of. It is a great gift to us each year that these little ones bring, often disguised as unruly behavior or a mysterious way of being that does not match our expectations.

There have been certain groups of children that I have had over the years that can be characterized as difficult groups, where there is conflict and unrest among the children. Sometimes it has manifested as a few children who seem to go out of their way to disturb each other—children who just can't get along with each other, bringing many days when there are bitter tears and angry voices—and sometimes it is the whole group that cannot find harmony. There are also groups of children where harmony prevails and the relationships are warm and loving. But more often we see that the group is a challenge—transitions fall into chaos, perhaps, or the children cannot hold form and there is tension in many of the relationships. Over the years I came to think of these groups of children as groups who rub the hard edges off each other, groups that are doing a social deed with each other. We can often see that where there is much conflict in a group one year, the next year these children are best of friends. But I also began to see, pretty early in my teaching, that they also come to rub the hard edges off of me, to make me socially more fit and capable, to deepen me as a teacher and as a human being. I became a better teacher through Natasha's sacrifice and through my failure; other times it has been through my striving that I have grown—striving to understand the inexplicable, to meet the child I do not understand, to be interested in who a child is rather than who I want that child to be. Children call upon us to be interested in them, to confront the mystery of their being with our striving. With sincere longing, with true effort on my part, I have felt that I am taking another baby step as a teacher and as a human being. In Chapter Two of *How to Know Higher Worlds* Rudolf Steiner reminds us that "for every one step you take in the pursuit of higher knowledge, take three steps in the perfection of your own character." This means we must be with others, for, to quote Goethe, "Talent develops in quiet places, character in the full current of human life."

It takes courage to walk into the classroom every day, to greet each child and parent with warmth, no matter what happened the day before. Each day must be like the first day of creation. Everything is possible, everything is becoming. It is a bit like the meditative life we strive to establish. We cannot have any goals. We never can get to the point when we can say, there, that's done. One starts anew each day. We often meet with no outer signs that signal any changes, with no defined goal, no guarantees, meeting the same challenges of yesterday, last week, last year, and often not feeling any different after our meditation than we did before. But day after day we try again. And each time we have the thought, as teachers, "Now I know how to be a teacher. Now I've got it," this is a guarantee that the next class will be difficult and once again we will know nothing. You will find that what you have done in the past will not work with this next group. The class is calling for you to do something different. I have a friend who once said to me, "When you see trouble coming down the road towards you, drop down on your knees and give thanks, for you are about to learn something important." I don't think I have gotten to that point yet, but I do recognize that there is something incredibly valuable in being challenged, in knowing nothing and starting over. When we are at our wits' end, we are the most open to inspiration, to intuition. As an Alzheimer's patient once said to me, in a lucid moment, "We do not have to know where we are to find ourselves there." When we don't know anything, we are poised to learn something, and when we feel helpless, we will be led to find a way to serve the other.

A friend had a class where everything was chaotic. This happened day after day. One day during cleanup it was so bad she stood in the middle of her class and did not know whether to cry or to leave. Then she had a moment of inspiration and looked into her pockets and said, "Oh, dear." Children began to gather. Then she said, "This is not good news. My dear children, I am sorry to say there is only this much [thumb and forefinger showing a tiny amount] patience left." The whole room changed.

Another colleague had an inspiration for a group that was very argumentative. Every day there were tears and confrontations. He walked to the children who were in tears and indignant and said, "It looks like

Old Man Trouble has been here again." Old Man Trouble began to be a presence in the classroom, objectifying the difficulties that were tempting the children to fall into unruly behavior. When the children began to argue, they would stop and say that Old Man Trouble was coming near.

We have to push ourselves into activity. We must work consciously with spiritual forces and work on our own inner development with great resolve. When I was a new teacher, my mentor said that an early childhood teacher has to be willing and able to sacrifice one's adult needs. In our adult lives, we crave stimulation, spontaneity, change, novelty, and we digest our experiences through talking; but these are not good things for our classroom. The rock we live on in our classrooms is rhythm and routine. These are cornerstones of each day. A good day in the classroom is one in which time ceases to exist and yet somehow, miraculously, we have snack at a reasonable time, circle and story flow, and the children are ready to go home when the parents arrive. We are quiet in the classroom, always doing tasks, and hopefully our every word and gesture is imbued with intentionality.

But we need to go deeper than this. We need to overcome adult attributes that we associate with modern-day adults—such as being critical, wanting to define and categorize, and wanting to fix. None of these will serve us in working with the children. We must free our thinking if we are to respond to the call of the future. With our thinking we can enter into the realm of ideas and ideals, and it is within our powers to be able to find the essential within these realms. Thinking is an active meditation, allowing us to be instigators of metamorphosis. If we can commit our thinking and feeling to something outside of ourselves, this will bring forth life-giving forces into our work. The more we can remove ourselves from sympathy and antipathy, the more easily can empathy arise in us. We need to develop what Henning Kohler describes as active tolerance.

When we have answers, it is an egotistical act that does not enter the reality of the other. Every child has a reason for incarnating as he has. If there is a hindrance, we can offer help and support but the child may or may not choose to change it. Active tolerance means that we leave others free to be themselves in all their individual expressions. It means we observe and think about them with gentle and unprejudiced interest and that we strive to understand them enough so that we can honor their way of being and behaving without judging them by our own standards or forcing them to meet our expectations.

Far too often we are reactive to life, including the children in our groups. Even after the first day of school, we can hear teachers saying "Oh, my goodness" about a child, a group, or a situation. Even if we think we have an ideal class, we are defining. It is important how we think about our children; they are particularly dependent upon our regard for them. The child's social development is aided by the fact that she lives into the soul life of the adults around her. Through ourselves we enable the connection between child and self. We are the self that the child is eventually able to find within herself.

In *Life Between Death and Rebirth*, Rudolf Steiner said, "For something to happen in the spiritual world, it is essential that there be absolute calmness of soul. The quieter we are, the more can happen through us in the spiritual world—that is what is creative in the spiritual world."[1] In calmness of soul we can learn how to respond rather than react. We can look at a child with an inner quiet that allows us to go from seeing to beholding. Perhaps a silly child is not being silly to annoy us or to disturb the class; perhaps his senses are so overloaded that he can do nothing else. A child who does not imitate may have been awakened too early into intellect and is paralyzed by living in a very chilly sheath. This child should not be sent out of the group but embraced in a warm soul environment. Most of the difficult behavior we see in the classroom is due to fear and pain. Every child wants to be seen by us and will show in his behavior where his difficulty lies. But it is up to us to learn that language. When we find fault, it is we who lack insight. We must ask whether a child can meet the expectations we have set. Wrong expectations have consequences; they can affect the child's self-concept for many years.

As early childhood teachers, we are soon forgotten and we may not see the fruits of our labors. When children move on to the grades, they can pass us in the hallways with no recognition. This is good, because the child has moved on, feeling at home in his group and looking towards the future, and we can rejoice for them. But in the early years our lives spill over into the lives of others and we are a kindling force and a revealing power in the lives of the children we have cared for. This life on earth is only a span of time in an endless spiral of striving; everything we do to help will help forever.

---

[1] Rudolf Steiner, *Life Between Death and Rebirth*, Lecture 4 (November 3, 1912, Vienna).

There is a wonderful verse by Herbert Hahn—

Remember daily that you are continuing the work of the spiritual world with the children.

You are the preparers of the path for these young souls who wish to form their lives in these difficult times.

The spiritual world will always stand by you in this task;

This is the wellspring of strength which you so need.[2]

What does this mean and how do we take up the challenge? Each night in sleep we meet spiritual beings, the hierarchies. Angels are beings who want to help us to form ideals and become capable of moral fantasy. They long to pour love into our souls. The child meets his higher I in sleep and with the angel's help learns to adapt himself to life. When a baby is awake, it is crying. Then it sleeps and goes back to the spiritual world from which it came. It is difficult to put an enormous being who lived outside of space and time into a child's tiny body. It takes many years for this relation [of soul/spirit and body] to fully form. But after a few months, the baby is awake more. It is finding its place in the body and responds with pleasure to being here. The angel carries out the archetypal, architectural plan of creation. Each night it works on the molding and configuring process which is so very active in the first years of life. The child feels the energizing and forming of the angel's hand. The angels take the child's body in hand, completely enclosing her, imparting to her with the utmost care and exactitude, the formative impulses to which her growth must adapt.

When the child comes out of sleep, out of a world where one breathes goodness, she expects the same tender care she experienced in the spiritual world. She expects to be cared for with dignity, patience and guidance. As the verse says, we are not alone. Higher beings want to be our partners. We can be their partners—and I believe that any successes we have in the classroom are due, in part, to this partnership—but we must not be self serving in this task. And here we must be very honest: are we asking for help so everyone will participate in our carefully prepared circle and listen to our story, to make our jobs easier? Or are we asking for help to ease a child's suffering? The child should feel that the help given to him streams from our acceptance and our completely tolerant attitude.

---

2 Quoted in "Birth to the Age of Three: Our Responsibility" by Dorothy Olsen, *Gateways* Issue 29.

We need to know how to form partnerships with these angelic beings. Rudolf Steiner said, "To have in our souls a lively image of the child's nature in every single year; nay, in every single week—this constitutes the spiritual basis of education."[3] We must prepare ourselves: exact and non-judgmental observation over time, forming clear thoughts with selfless interest and being involved enough, inwardly, with the children to such an extent that we can feel tenderness for their challenges. We must formulate our questions with care and form a living image of the child. It is a very thorough preparation; but if we do it, the higher beings will always respond.

On September 9, 1919, Rudolf Steiner gathered together the first twelve Waldorf teachers for the first time. He gave the teachers a means for making connection with the spiritual world. He said to them, "In the evening before your meditation, ask the angels, archangels, and archai that they may help you in your work the following day." He was asking them to open themselves in such a way that spiritual substance could pour itself into their soul beings: into their will, their feeling and their thinking. In doing this, the basis for imagination, inspiration, and intuition is created. Then Rudolf Steiner shook each teacher's hand and looked deeply into his eyes, as if sealing a sacred pledge. We, too, must take this pledge; it is the ground upon which we stand as Waldorf educators. This *is* the wellspring of strength of which we so stand in need.

I once had a conversation with my daughter, who was considering having a child. I told her that I hoped she would become a mother because I had had such joy in being a parent and wanted the same for her. My generation will not always be active anymore, though many of us have many more years of activity. I am aware that I am passing the torch, placing it in the hands of those who will carry it into the future. I feel a bit as I did in this conversation with my daughter; how rich and full it will be for you and how you will grow and blossom amidst all the hard work and effort!

I visit many early childhood programs in many parts of the world each year and there are also things I see that give me grave concerns. In the spirit of passing this torch, I would like to offer some kindly advice.

---

3 Rudolf Steiner, *The Spiritual Ground of Education*, Lecture 1 (August 16, 1922, Oxford).

Waldorf education runs the risk of becoming mechanical, as we increasingly put our trust in outer appearances rather than inner activity. We are placing too much emphasis on the environment—with the pink lazured walls, silk cloths, and wooden toys—and not enough trust in the inner activity. We are not studying and not meditating. With Rudolf Steiner it was a given that every teacher would have a well-developed meditative life to accompany her teaching. We are increasingly taking up the artistic activities of the classroom in the spirit of, "because that is what we do in a Waldorf kindergarten." We are losing the thinking behind why we do these things. I have been in countries where everyone, in every school, is doing the same circle at the same time of year. I have seen boxes in the cupboards marked "Harvest Nature Table," or "Advent decorations." This is an artistic education, demanding of us that we be artists in every realm. We must be creative and create anew each year. Teaching out of convention, out of habit, is one of the three enemies to Waldorf education.[4]

We are masters of beauty; we know how to create beauty. But our classrooms are becoming a bit too precious. In some classrooms one feels that one cannot breathe because things are so perfect. Who is the teacher doing this for? Is it out of the teacher's own need for order or is it something for the children? All too easily, our classrooms can become the cozy world of the teacher and not the world of the child. Sometimes things are so perfect that the only thing for the children to do is to destroy the perfection. We become guardians of our "nests" and guard them from others—parents, colleagues and even from the children, instead of creating environments that invite the children into relational activity. Our need for control can become stronger than our desire to work out of a sound pedagogical base and much damage can

---

4 Louise recalled these "enemies" as being attributed to a statement by Rudolf Steiner in a lecture by Heinz Zimmermann, but we have not been able to find this lecture. Steiner spoke in several places of three similar dangers of our time, for example in *The Younger Generation*, Lecture 4 (October 7, 1922): "In our time the soul must strive beyond empty phrase, convention and routine; beyond the empty phrase to a grasp of truth; beyond convention to a direct, elementary warm-hearted relation between man and man; beyond routine to the state in which the Spirit lives in every single action, so that we no longer act automatically but that the Spirit lives in the most ordinary everyday actions. We must come to spirituality in action, to the immediate experience of human beings in their relations to one another and to honest, upright experience of truth." However, there is no mention of "enemies of Waldorf education" in this passage or in any others we have been able to find. We would be grateful for any help in tracing this reference.

be done. Too often we are removing children from the activity because we are uncomfortable, not because it is in the best interest of the child. In some schools, the teachers are desperately trying to keep everyone happy—children, parents and colleagues—at the expense of the goals of the education on behalf of the child. This is acting out of set routines, the second enemy of Waldorf education.

We are teaching more and more out of direct instruction rather than imitation. We need to put our faith in our education and trust in the wisdom of anthroposophy. Often this instruction is sung, "Get on your coat, Sit in your chair..." thinking that, since we are singing, we are not really giving instructions. Even sung in mood of the fifth, it is still direct instruction. Believe in imitation. Have faith that the children will follow what we do. We will be surprised to find that it actually works. We must hold ourselves to the same standard that we hold the children to. Transform yourself in becoming the model for rightful relationships, moral activity and trust, not only in the children, but in the goodness and the rightfulness of the world. We have all had the extreme good fortune of coming into contact with the thoughts of Rudolf Steiner in this lifetime. With that privilege also comes a responsibility. We must take anthroposophy personally! We need to trust Waldorf education, for if we do not, who will?

Allow yourselves to live with questions rather than answers. Have genuine interest in the parents and listen to them more than talk. Be interested in the world but jump to no conclusions. Look behind appearances to find the truth. Speak in such a way that everyone can understand you and always listen for common ground: for the third enemy of Waldorf education is set phrases and having all the answers. Do not be content with being; strive to become.

In closing, I would like to share with you some thoughts from Mother Theresa:

> *We need to love without getting tired. How does a lamp burn?*
> *Through the continuous input of small drops of oil.*
> *What are these drops of oil in our lamps?*
> *They are the small things of daily life:*
> *Faithfulness, small words of kindness, a thought for others,*
> *Our way of being silent, of looking, of speaking, of acting.*[5]

---

5 Mother Teresa, *No Greater Love* (New World Library, 2001), p. 22.

From Unbornness to I-Consciousness
The Three Great Steps of Incarnation
~ **Dr. Michaela Glöckler, Switzerland**

There are three steps for "I"-consciousness awareness to find its place in the physical body. How does this happen? We constantly experience "I"-awareness as a point [a large dot as "point" was drawn on the blackboard]; and if we don't succeed in focusing, concentrating, so that we become totally present with ourselves, we are not really there. We have to "be there" to look at the complexity of this world and make it clear to ourselves, the world of thoughts, feelings, of our striving, of what we want to do and are not able to do because of something in our way. There is all this richness, this wealth. On the other hand there are the complex conditions of our life—one billion people are starving; they live with the minimum. Someone else has too much to eat, and those in between ask what planet we are on here where this can be tolerated. Rudolf Steiner said calmly that the social question is a pedagogical question. And the pedagogical question is a medical question. If you don't know what is healthy and what is sick, how can you recognize the healthful aims of education?

Another statement of Rudolf Steiner is that in the future, people will not ask what is true or false but about what is healthy and what is sick. What is healthy? What is unhealthy? Physicians can define that well. Healthy is being master of possibilities. Sick is not being master and being unable to unfold one's possibilities. Health is being able to serve. Sickness is being limited, restricted from serving. And that is a question of education. How do we have to incarnate so we become an instrument for ourselves and for others too, so that we humanize and do not dehumanize? When we can do this, we will be able to solve the social question. We can also advance possibilities for others. This is the possibility surrounding a young child. The young child is obviously in need of support, and the whole surroundings become centered on the child and on his need for development. We want to please the little child and make him happy. Sometimes we do this with sweets, but it is better to do it through a smile.

But we need a concept of what is healthy self-awareness, self-consciousness. Everything around me, the world in which I am, finds itself within me and finds a point in me from which I can relate to the outer world without losing myself. With all this wealth of feelings and thoughts, it is amazing that we do not lose ourselves. All this is the gift of the physical body. In the physical body self-awareness awakens. The whole world of wisdom finds itself. I have my balance point, my center of gravity. And it is on that balance point that my spiritual center of gravity forms, so that I can sense myself in one point. Then around this point there is my destiny [a large circle was drawn with the point as its center].

Rudolf Steiner states in his lectures on occult investigations into the life between death and rebirth[1] that an incarnating soul knows that for the next earth life he needs a certain kind of education. The soul needs a certain kind of knowledge that he can absorb early on. But often this education is needed at a time of childhood when we do not have the parents that would offer us a happy life. And if we go to parents who might not give us a happy life, when we would prefer different parents, then this education which we may not be able to reach becomes the most important thing. One cannot imagine all the different situations that incarnating souls experience in spiritual life.

One finds souls who before birth had the most terrible struggle in themselves because they saw that they might be abused in youth by a horrible set of parents. We see many souls who go through terrible struggles in the spiritual world as they proceed toward the preparation of their births. This is not only an inner struggle but is also projected to the outside and one has the struggles outside oneself as well. The souls go to their next incarnation feeling a deep split within. Rudolf Steiner

---

[1] Rudolf Steiner, *Life Between Death and Rebirth* (selections from GA 140).

describes a situation of looking ahead to preview the coming incarnation. We know that the soul prepares for a particular generation, country, language, parents, and so on. But now because of interference with birth (through abortion), hundreds of thousands of girls, especially, are murdered. These souls then have to orient themselves to decide if they want to come. Souls are constantly rejected and sent back.

Then there is the additional struggle to decide between a happy family life and educational constellation or a horrible one. Therefore one of the messages of this lecture is to encourage the founding of new kindergartens. New care centers will be founded in our towns so that the right education will be available to these children who will not get to come in to the proper situation in their families. I once encountered a beautiful founding of a Waldorf school, where parents put an ad in the local paper saying that they wanted to found a Waldorf school in their community. "Come to the pub." Thirty people came and then ten founded the school. The more places there are for a good education, the easier it will be for the unborn souls to find the right incarnating possibilities for themselves.

[Returning to the chalk drawing] This circle is our destiny. It has a wide aspect as well. We are constantly in conversation with our destiny, which is our partner, the sphere with which we have to converse.

Destiny is the horizon with which we are always in dialogue. The more we have this dialogue about its meaning, about the positive side of what we can learn from it, especially in very difficult destiny situations, the better it will be for our "I"-consciousness. There is a wonderful statement from medieval mysticism—"I do not know who I am, I do not know what I know." I am a strange thing, a dot and a circle. I only unfold a healthy "I"-awareness when I am point and circle, becoming aware of myself in my body and developing the ability to have this conversation with my destiny, the developmental chance I have when I bring point and circle so together that attention is brought together for the unfolding of my biography.

There are three great steps into incarnation. The third step does not have to do with our dialogue partner of destiny. It has to do with our true essence, our true persona, the being that resounds through the body and through the soul—how we feel, think and act. Always something radiates through of the essence of a person, the radiation of her persona. What radiates through is love. Our destiny is tied to the astral body, ether body and physical body. Everything is inscribed into them, depending on what we have done that is good or difficult. All these consequences are drawn onto the paper or sand of these bodies. Our "I," however, did not experience the fall from paradise, and remains innocent, pure. It is pure love; pure light; the Way, the Truth, and the Life. Our "I" holds within it the goddesses we are seeing each morning of this conference in eurythmy.[2] If we look at the male virtues of vigor and courage and add these as well, there are expressions of "I" that are neither male nor female. The "I" can bring different properties to expression through a male body than a female one. It also depends upon what the world around us allows us to do, what is possible for our gender, as for example in China or Peru. If there are no partners to share our destiny with, we reserve our possibilities for another incarnation.

Radiating and holding back are the two sides. The body is a carrier of the "I"-consciousness and it is a carrier of developmental possibilities. Both are there.

There are two beings, Lucifer and Ahriman, who do not like these components at all. Lucifer does not want us to have awareness of the world around us. He wants us to enjoy ourselves, mirror ourselves, and develop aberrations from healthy self-awareness that go toward egoism. Like Lilith, we are not so nice as women if Lucifer tempts us. Men can do this in their own way. This is where Luciferic temptation comes in. Lucifer is a microcosm interested in small things. Lucifer is happy with vanity. Life has to be fun and joyful, where we can take pride in ourselves and show off. Rudolf Steiner once came onto the school playground in Stuttgart and said that there were two ladies sitting in front of the school who could not be allowed in. A teacher who went to look saw no one. But Rudolf Steiner explained that the two he saw sitting there were vanity and the craving for power.

Ahriman, on the other hand, has a deep hatred and lack of understanding for destiny. People are only numbers to him. Everyone is exchangeable to him. Schiller described through the inquisitor in *Don Carlos* that people are just numbers. Rudolf Steiner told physicians that Ahriman wants to kill karma. We cannot use a more accurate concept. We have to listen to it and ponder on it. Ahriman wants to kill destiny because it makes development possible. Grand Ahrimanic powers focus on the

---

2 A eurythmy performance represented a series of goddesses going from Isis (Egyptian), Layla (Iranian / Sufi), Lakshmi (Indian), Kore (Greek), Lilith (Hebrew), Banshee (Celtic), to Sophia (Russian).

earth, on the solid, the rational, the mathematical. Of course we cannot live without these; all this is his work. But Ahriman wants us to use these powers to dominate and control others. Lucifer and Ahriman cannot understand development, which is a Christian, human, humane motif.

Therefore the third aspect of incarnation is that the persona is always in dialogue with these two powers. Ahriman works with hatred and envy. Lucifer works with enjoyment, pleasure, and vanity. If we keep these in mind, we understand what is essential. The true persona, the human principle, works with love, dignity and freedom. If I am not constantly in danger of doing something wrong, I cannot find out for myself what is right. We learn from mistakes and doing so is always a victory over Lucifer and Ahriman. There is nothing more Christian than making mistakes. If we feel stupid because we have made a mistake and resolve to do better, then feelings of inner strength come. We practice and practice and overcome Ahriman, because we devote our time to improving ourselves and do not try to dominate others. Then what arises is an atmosphere around children where they experience that the world is good.

I was so pleased last night when Louise deForest spoke of kindergartens that are too perfect. But there are also "oh dear!" kindergartens where the educators do not understand the requirements of sensory development. It is important that we know why we do what we do, why the walls are a certain color, for example. When each experience that greets the children is consciously chosen we can feel joy each morning that what surrounds us is good for the children. We radiate our joy in knowing what is good. We must add to the outer experience an understanding of what it stands for, with a commitment to thoroughly know what we are doing. We combine light, air, color, form and enough space to be flexible. We also allow moments of intentional chaos, so that we can all find our way back to form. Then the children will be able to feel the process toward development.

Taking hold of the body, looking toward destiny from pre-earthly life, and developing "I"-awareness are all things that we need to do. Taking hold of the body is the first step of incarnating.

The second step addresses our karmic surroundings. As much as we can, we have to form the child's environment so that he feels addressed, accepted, and taken into a world where people communicate with one another.

Then with the third step of incarnation can come the flash of "I am." Here comes the first shining experience of "I am." I have a body; I have a destiny. But I am not just these. I am more. I am a being. The more my body becomes an instrument of my development, and my destiny the arena of my development, the better my "I" can find itself.

In the human ovum we see a point surrounded by a circle. The image of the ovum looks as though it has a subtly glowing corolla around the circumference. The next image of a solar eclipse [not shown] looks very similar. Here we have the microcosm and the macrocosm. Only the sizes are different. But the movements of the stars up in the heavens are the same rhythms, the same movements active in the physical evolution of the body. [To further illustrate this reflection of the macrocosm/microcosm, the image of a developing sun out in some galaxy, with its swirling, spiraling shape, was shown alongside that of the developing tissue fibers of the heart.]

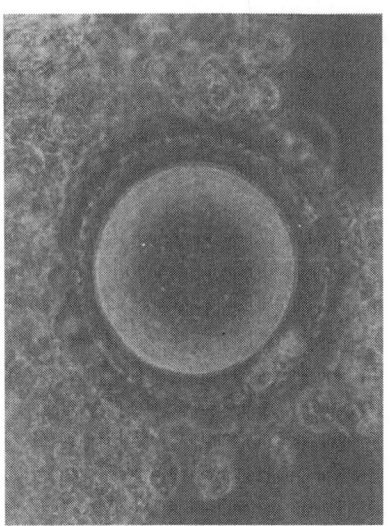

A human egg cell. Image from Gertrude Lux Flanagan, *The First Nine Months of Life*

A developing sun

26 ~ Michaela Glöckler

The developing heart organ is similar because the fibers move in the same kind of vortex pattern as the developing sun. This cosmic swirling pattern is also seen in human fingerprints. We see these motifs again in the development of children's drawings. [The spiraling condenses to a point that becomes enclosed by a circle.]

After fertilization, there is the tiny hovering of a point forming within the liquid of the amnion, surrounded by the circle of the trophoblast. The play between the inner and the outer continues with the development of the ear and eye. The ear is a wonderful spiral that goes entirely inside. When we hear we internalize. The eye goes out and becomes global. Rudolf Steiner observed these similarities.

There is dramatic play of forces from week to week that creates the organ systems in such a way that they work well together. The organs develop first. Only then do the limbs begin to take shape. The limbs are inserted into the physical body from the outside. The head evolves from the center. The "destiny" person, the person of action, comes from the periphery. [The forming of the limbs from the periphery was demonstrated by a series of photos that show just the little buds that will develop into hands and feet. By gradual steps, indentations appear in the buds which begin to differentiate into fingers and toes. The shape of the fingers and toes appears to be impressed upon the hands and feet from the outside.]

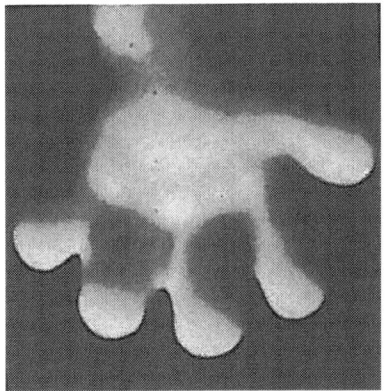 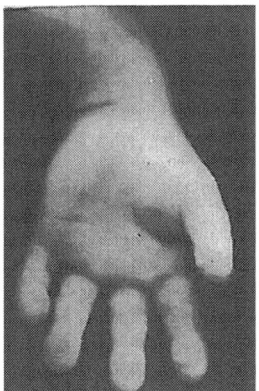

Two stages of hand development in utero (*The First Nine Months of Life*)

Then the child is born and enters independently into the physical world. The child is freed from the mother's narrow body. This first liberation opens the doorway to more freedom. Every learning process is a bit of liberation. Learning something new gives us more freedom for the

From Unbornness to I–Consciousness 27

future because we have learned something new to use. Aborigines say that initiation is always when we learn something new. In the Shinto tradition, a new initiation occurs every two-and-two-thirds years, just as Rudolf Steiner saw. [Something unique to human beings was demonstrated in a slide showing the arrangement of human teeth.] The child and adult have the same size and shape of gum and positioning for the first ten teeth. This does not change with the loss and replacement of the baby teeth. This allows the human being to speak. In animals, it is not the same. The teeth and the jaw change with growth. [A slide showed how a baby chimpanzee's face and jaw are similar in profile to a human child. But as the chimp matures, the jaw becomes much more prominent and thrust forward.]

The more specialized something becomes, the less it is free. There is less freedom for the being to meet the world with. Animals grow apart from the human being and specialize themselves. With our arms we cannot fly like birds, but we can do so many other things. Waldorf education wants to educate toward freedom. That means as much as possible in early childhood the first years of school should be without specialization. Then the human instrument has more possibilities. Then there is no one-sidedness, and the more human and less animal-like we will be.

When we speak, the glottis is closed. When we breathe, it opens. We stop breathing when we speak. Parallel to this is brain development. It is a stormy activity. Everything we bring to the child from the outside stimulates development.

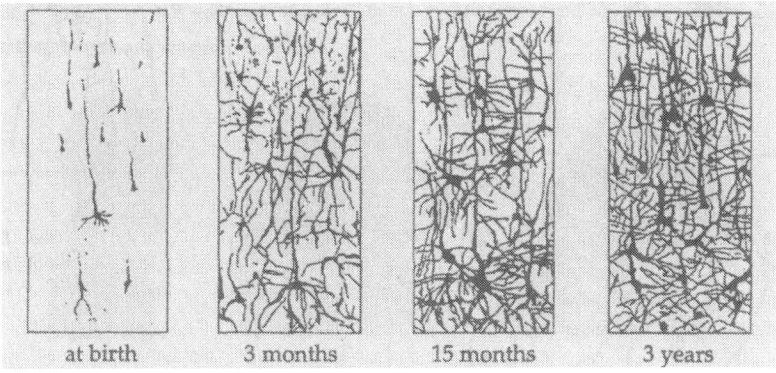

Microscopic sections of the human cerebrum showing synapses between brain cells. From M. Glöckler, S. Langhammer, C. Wiechert: *Education – Health for Life*.

[A slide illustrated this stormy picture of development. Pictures of nerve fibers in the brain were shown from the newborn through the ages of 3, 15, and 24 months.] The brain becomes increasingly complex and chaotic-looking in this pattern of complexity.

What is happening within the brain is caused by the experience of outside stimuli meeting the child. This is all unconscious preparation for the persona. This physical instrument will be the physical home of the "I" that can meet others. [This thought ended with a photo of a little child walking along behind two adults. The child is walking with head bowed and hands clasped behind his back in exact imitation of the two men.]

We carry the laws of the cosmos within us, which direct how we form ourselves. But there is also an aspect of our higher being that is always in communication with the hierarchies. This can express itself in different ways. How can we meet our different children in their different development of self-awareness? If we take seriously these three steps, we can become masters of the physical body, of physical development. But we can also be experts of destiny. For ten to fifteen mintues in each faculty meeting we should read lectures on reincarnation and karma and lectures about life between death and new birth.

Why? This is the world where the "I" decides to come back to the earth. This is the world where beings communicate with other beings, where our "I" is connected with the dead, with the elemental beings, with the angelic hierarchies, the divinity, the trinity that forms our body in its image, differentiating it into three parts. We are images of the divine essence. If we study lectures on destiny we understand that whatever we do in one life to improve radiates back in next life in more healthy body and more harmonious destiny. Then we can become citizens of two worlds. With the children we can give them a helm in spirit, soul, and body. We all keep Natasha [mentioned by Louise deForest in her opening lecture as the child she has learned most from because she feels that she failed her] in our minds as the potential for our learning.

Event of Destiny	Consequences for the current biography or a later earthly life
Benevolence	The person feels healthy, radiates soul warmth, everything succeeds better and more easily. Adroitness in the following incarnation.
Contentment	Wounds heal better. The person finds it easier to keep an even keel in life, and has a harmonious effect on his surroundings.
Acting out of love	causes much joy and warmth to come to one in the next life. It gives life wings. In the life after next, the person has the gift of understanding Mankind and the world more easily. The person has a free, open sense for the world.
Lack of love	harms the astral body of the other person.
If someone could imitate meaningful activities out of his own free incentive as a preschooler and was not forced to conform to rules	he can more easily maintain health and freshness even to an advanced age, and will repeatedly be able to find the inner strength to start something new.
If someone is prevented as a preschooler from following his inner needs in action and imitation,	the soul is more easily depleted in the course of life, and the physical infirmities of old age are more likely to come to the fore.
A school-aged child before puberty who could look up to individuals as loved authorities, who felt reverence for the wonders of nature, who could learn to reverently pray,	posesses self-understood authority later in life and can have a helpful, indeed blessing effect on his community through his mere presence. He is inclined to establish a personal relationship to truth.
Interest in the sense world	creates a disposition for a rich life of soul in the next lifetime, and a healthy body in the lifetime after that.

The capacities, talents, handicaps of one earth life	are carried into our physical/etheric organization in the next life, and they cause an inner disposition to health and illness.
Remains of a former, not entirely dissolved astral body from a past life	can under certain destined circumstances become a false, invalid "Guardian of the Threshold" in bad dreams and visions that trouble the "I" like a second "I." This guardian can easily emerge from the current members of the human being and appear as a double.

Events of Destiny and Future Temperaments

If someone had to be alone a lot and was forced to move in the smallest of circles and developed little interest in other people	A tendency to become a melancholic in the next life
If someone experienced a lot, went many places, could connect with people, but also had to accept rough treatment and put up with this	A disposition for a choleric temperament
A pleasant, easy life in which much was seen and looked at	A disposition for a phlegmatic and sanguine temperament

Charts translated from M. Glöckler: *Begabung und Behinderung* (Freies Geistesleben 2004), based on the karmic research of Rudolf Steiner, in

Theosophy (GA 9)

Manifestations of Karma (GA 120)

Karmic Relationships, vol. 1-8 (GA 235-240)

Die Verbindung zwischen Lebenden und Toten (GA 168)

Wege und Ziele des geistigen Menschen. Lebensfragen im Lichte der Geisteswissenschaft (GA 125)

The I, the Self, and the Body
Steps Going Up and Steps Going Down

∼ **Dr. Edmond Schoorel, Netherlands**

A photo taken on a Dutch island sand dune was the opening image for this lecture. It shows nature—sand and dune grasses—with a little bit of culture—a ring of stumps placed by a 19-year-old boy as part of his senior project. The student created this as a place of contemplation. Here we see both a natural, raw setting along with the influences that an outer impulse—the student creating the ring of stumps—placed in the setting. This image introduces the consideration of the two streams the lecture will consider—that which is innate to the setting or individual and that which approaches from the outside and the future. Dr. Schoorel expressed thanks to the student for allowing this photo to be shown.

As you think upon your own experiences, do you recognize this? You have prepared a wonderful program for your group, your class, or your child's birthday party. Everything is well thought out and well prepared. And then suddenly something happens that messes up everything. It storms and rains while you prepared the party for outside. There are extra children in your class because your colleague got sick. Or the helper for the birthday party has called to say she cannot come. The whole plan is changed, but then you have to improvise.

Yesterday in Dr. Glöckler's lecture we heard about the difficult choices souls have to make in arranging their path into incarnation. Improvising is the normal situation for a child who comes to earth. Children carefully prepare. They choose the country, the culture, the language, parents and other people they want to meet. But the reality then turns out to be that the parents they have chosen are getting divorced, the school is shutting down, the best karmic friend is moving away. The child needs to improvise all the time in the incarnating process. Most children can cope with this; they have the possibility in their physiology to do this, though the circumstances may be difficult. We will speak today of the physiology of the predictable and the unpredictable in development, steps going up and down.

Threefoldness
First we will look at two incarnating routes before working them out. The threefold human being is the starting point with the upper pole, rhythmic area, and lower pole. Rudolf Steiner gives these three areas double names: the nerve-sense area/upper pole, metabolic-limb area/lower pole, and in between, the area of rhythmic processes—breathing and circulation.

As well as these three different domains, humans also have two opposite incarnating routes within them, one that represents the past and one that opens the door to the future. We can recognize how past and future streams are illustrated when we look at a child's developmental stages. Children must stand upright, an innate capacity from the past, before they can walk. The ability to listen must exist before they can learn to speak. And children must have thoughts before they can identify what they perceive. But developing these abilities is not automatic. Around the child must be adults and children who already walk, speak, and think, to become imitative models for the child, so that the future can come to efficacy. In their own individual situations, children will develop themselves as members of a language community and become participants in the common human world of thoughts. By observing the created world that we all have in common, they learn to speak for themselves and to act in the group that they belong to. From this point they can then do things individually because of who they uniquely are; this expresses the individual. For most children, this happens without difficulty. But for some others the development falters and they get stuck along these routes and may need therapy.

Twofoldness
The human being comes to earth along two routes. One proceeds from below upward, ending in the head, and comes from the past. This route we associate with wisdom. The other one flowing from the head downward is oriented toward the future, ends in the pelvic region, and makes us think of light. There is one stream that is common to us all, the upward stream that enables us to stand, listen, and think— and another part that is individual, expressed in walking, speaking, and perceiving the world, which flows from the head downward.

The stream going up
Let us begin with looking at the upward stream. This we may call the stream of thinking, seeing that it ends up in the head. Out of the breadth of pre-natal life, human beings prepare their landing on earth. They do not do it alone but have high, hierarchical helpers. The person directing this process is not the person we meet casually on the street later on but is the spiritual being within oneself to whom we later say "I." All the wisdom gained in previous incarnations, as well as the wisdom that created humanity overall, works during pregnancy. From the periphery, both universal forces and individual formative forces from the I give humans the strength to condense, to compact themselves. The developing human being pulls itself in from the embryonic sheath so the child can physically appear on earth. The embryonic sheaths, comprised of the placenta, amnion, chorion, and the amniotic fluid, are beautiful images of the nurturing, supporting power of growth of the upward stream. From the moment of birth these physical sheaths are no longer needed and fall away. Their functions are taken over by the up-going stream. A big change at birth is that the I no longer works on the inside of the human body but takes the lead from outside. After birth the I of day consciousness takes over guiding development. At night the upward stream can still do its work and aids recovery processes. When we follow the upward stream on its route, we first find the metabolic system—the source of substance formation, the source of vitality. The astral body dominates the upward stream and works in various organs. Incredibly

high star wisdom works in the human body because we have organs.

Continuing upward, the diaphragm forms a boundary to the rhythmic system where we find the seven life processes. One of these seven processes is breathing. Breathing provides us with an appropriate picture for the events in this area. In breathing there is a rhythmic exchange between inside and outside. Breathing makes the difference between being alive or not. In the same way that metabolism is the source of substance, the rhythmic system is the source of life. In the rhythmic area, the astral body is no longer supreme. The astral body has left its imprint in organs below the diaphragm. In the rhythmic system the ether body is the ruler and works in rhythms. That is also why this area is interwoven with rhythms.

The stream going up is becoming more and more barren. We left the I outside the physical body, the astral body below the diaphragm, and the etheric body below the neck. In the head only the physical body's primary effect is in charge. The ego, astral body, and etheric body have left their imprints in the physical head at an earlier time. When we try to find them, we can discover the intentions of the I, the wisdom of the astral body, and the living images of the etheric body inscribed in our thinking head. In the head, the dynamic of the upward stream comes to a standstill, becomes crystallized, and congeals into images, about which we can think. The physical body, too, forms an imprint in the whole skeleton and in the brain. This fact—that the physical body makes an imprint—gives us the feeling that we are who we are, every day the same person. The skeleton and brain are the physical imprint of the I. The skeleton is slightly more lifeless than the brain. We might formally say that the up stream dies in the head.

The stream going down
Now we come to the unpredictable side of development. The stream going down has a different mood. When we want to describe it properly, we need to conform to this mood. Day awakens. The rooster crows, the alarm goes off, a full bladder—or maybe, alas, a wet bed—awakens the child. Children wake up differently—some quickly, some struggling to get into bodies that give a lot of resistance. A splash of cold water in the faces and a good breakfast help in waking up.

At the start of a new day the senses also wake up. Strictly speaking, the child arrives on earth every day anew and comes into the created world, the sensory world. The moment of waking up is related to the moment of birth. He comes from a world of creative will to the world of senses, which is full of sound, color, taste, and smell. The child feels deeply related to this world, which pulls him awake through the twelve bridges of his senses. All sensory experience has its impact on the child's soul. Sensory experiences form the child down to the level of the physical body. In the nerve-sense pole there is strong collaboration between the senses and the brain. The imprints upon the physical body of the upward stream are partly determined by what is presented to them by the perceptions of the senses belonging to the downward stream.

After breakfast, the day can start. What shall we do today? We go down one step of the downward stream to the rhythmic area of social experience. Who is around, is there someone to play with, is it a school day or home day? While chatting, pushing, laughing, and grumbling, the child emerges as a fellow human being within his group. Through life experience the child learns how things work. This takes energy; the children get tired and are ready for a nap.

We can call this downward stream a will stream if we look to its end point—meaning the actual deeds, not the force of will which belongs to the upward stream. When does the child begin to act, to express its will? A screaming, hungry baby is expressing will and is usually successful. A hollering toddler that has been startled expresses will. A six-year-old who makes a cute face to get what she wants expresses something in her behavior. Will here is quite selfish. But from a very young age the child can also be unselfish by not crying when he sees his mummy sad or by sharing toys to comfort another child.

The region below the diaphragm is a puzzling area. Why do children act so differently from each other? Is it not precisely in how a child acts that something very personal emerges? Children come from the prenatal world with specific intentions. Through their fellow human beings they meet their fate. We can say that this is the outside of fate. In the upward stream the karmic inside of fate is hidden as capabilities, as possibilities. These capabilities want to become visible, want to be fulfilled. Who does that? It is the downward stream. How do children get the idea to do certain things? By meeting others. What does this look like? It is through their behavior, their deeds towards others that they fulfill their possibilities: the hug, the bad temper, the step forward in development are all examples. The downward stream magically summons the I to appear by means of the deeds.

To be precise, it is not the I that appears here but the personality. By personality is meant the ego, the self. There is much confusion about the terms I, ego, self, personality, individuality, higher ego, superego, lower self. That is not the point here. What is meant is this. The way people show themselves in everyday life we will call personality. Not all possibilities humans bring to earth will emerge. In terms of the two streams, the down-stream makes something visible of the possibilities of the up-stream. Future and past work together to shape the unique personality. This demonstrates itself in the upper pole of the human body in the manner of how people perceive things. In the rhythmic system we can see this in the style of being of fellow humans. In the lower pole it demonstrates itself in people's deeds. In the downward will stream we see the day-conscious I at work. The I in the downward stream can use its forces to resolve aspects it meets in the astral, etheric, and physical bodies flowing toward it from the up-stream.

Cooperation between the two streams
So far I have mentioned several ways in which the upward stream and downward stream cooperate in the threefold human organism. I want to elaborate now on this cooperation further to show its developmental possibilities. In the upper pole the sense organs work together with the brain. The beginning of the downward stream co-operates with the endpoint of the upward stream. Where the future enters on its journey (to eventually emerge in the redemptive forces of deeds), it meets the silent images of the past. What are the developmental possibilities between these two? When the silent images of the thinking head find a connection to the world of ideas, to the wisdom of the astral world, people will get pictures that become alive. Instead of abstract images they will have lively pictures. The human being can become aware that thoughts have a connection to the world of ideas. When people look out of their eyes while carrying these lively pictures, they will perceive much more. They will discover the creative idea, the creative force behind sense-perceptible reality.

This is not something for the distant future. The preschoolers around whom this conference revolves are already doing this; they are clear-perceiving, clairvoyant. They perceive reality at the same time that they have sensory impressions, but are not yet aware of what they perceive. The sensory world is still transparent. Conversely, when the reality of the perceived world works on the silent images of the upper pole, these are released from their semblance-like character and we can say, "Oh, is that what it is?" By thinking, we can bring an idea into the reality of the sense world. Little children do not think much, but what they think has the character of discovering something. In his teacher the child sees the archetype of all teachers, not just anybody.

In the rhythmic area, collaboration takes place on a feeling level. Looking at conversation may help to illustrate this. In conversation there is an alternation between speaking and listening. We speak on exhalation and listen on inhalation. We can see these two types of children before us. One type is noisy in the speaking and is in the "send" mode all of the time. Then there are the shy, listening, receiving children whom we might easily lose sight of. When cooperation between speaking and listening goes well, the way the other person listens changes. Listening becomes less passive and increasingly more active. The receiver no longer feels overwhelmed and the speaker feels understood. The speaker does not feel the need to express himself so much. Judging becomes milder. Words and opinions become more and more imbued by what they will trigger in the other's soul. Children are already able to develop this in their play. In playing together, children carry on this mysterious, magic-realistic conversation through their shared fantasy world. We adults can learn a lot from the children.

What does this look like in the lower pole? A crying baby demonstrates the power of the metabolism. Everyone has seen children get their way, boys often forcefully, girls sometimes with manipulation and cunning. We can see the coarseness of the will and know that has not yet been cultivated. We are used to this in children and take pedagogical measures to channel this wild force somewhat in the right direction. The biggest task for a child is to learn cooperation between the metabolism and his or her deeds. We want to help the child guide impulsiveness. And it would be nice if this wildness, this unrestrained power would let itself be guided. This is a picture of the so-called ADHD child. These children have an advantage when they can learn to use power and speed for a purpose beyond themselves. The wildness may become instrumental for a greater purpose. But here we touch on a great moral problem, for the children can also be instruments for ignoble intentions. A number of these so-called ADHD children end up in delinquency.

What can the genius of a skilled deed learn from metabolism? Earlier this morning we mentioned that the upward stream carries the results of earlier experience, of both the universal human and of the individual past. In the lower pole, these are present in a pure, all-encompassing, omnipotent fashion. These are kernels of karma waiting to germinate. In the upper pole, we encountered them as pictures. In the metabolic-limb system, they are seeds, they are reminiscences. If conditions are favorable in these situations, the child can learn new motives to act upon and not just go for: "What the eyes see, the little hands want to grab." The child and we together are going to do something that is for the good of all, bringing us further. This is what all of you educators are doing all day.

The younger the children are, the more the universal human principles, such as learning to stand upright, learning to connect to the language genius, gaining access to thinking, are at stake. Already when a child takes his first steps, the personality begins to reveal itself. Why does the child walk? To meet his destiny. What environment can support this destination? In the three great steps of walking, speaking, and thinking, children climb up to the stillness of the head. Also in three steps children take hold of their bodies from heaven downwards, into the dynamics of the abdomen. There they are emerging on earth, acting in the physical world.

Threats

What are things that threaten the child's development? It is not right to deny the opposing forces a voice. After all, they enable human development towards freedom and love. Let's look again at the threefold human organism. Looking to the upper / nerve-sense pole, we see we have virtual reality in the world of screens. These are illusions, not real pictures. If we want to help the child meet the world of thought as a reality, we need to restrain screen use and encourage reflection. In our world of haste and multi-tasking, this has become very difficult.

In the rhythmic area, what has become of good conversations, active listening, and mild judgments? When there is no real community building and others speak to my inner world, my body must defend itself. We see this happen in the epidemic spread of high sensitivity and allergy conditions. The child must guard and defend itself against involuntary, external influences in different ways: physically through eczema and psychologically through fear. Children are asked to give opinions and are rewarded for early judgments, for lack of restraint, which encourages precocious development. Social status as a child is measured by the number of friends at the birthday party. Is this community building?

In the lower pole, strength in this region can take two directions. Some children resign themselves and no longer find their source of strength and vitality. This can manifest as chronic fatigue syndrome. This used to be for older children. Now even preschoolers are chronically tired. On the other hand, this discharge of strength in the lower pole can also show as aggression, hatred, and ruthlessness. We can see this being encouraged as parents incite their child to action on the soccer field. On the other side we see rules, protocols, student tracking, and tests, so the children know what to do and will do as they should. We train the children to become machines. We will also see headstrong children who go their own way—"You're not my boss!" Computer games encourage this barging ahead, in which morality is put on the back burner.

Christ between Lucifer and Ahriman
As we look at our present situation, we can become discouraged. We see Lucifer and Ahriman as powerful, opposing forces; but that is semblance. It looks like a perfect partnership with Ahriman reigning supreme in the upward stream; Lucifer is at home in the downward stream. In both poles they reach for each other. Lucifer is fond of illusion and can continue work on Ahriman's false images in thinking. Ahriman loves selfishness of the will and likes self-interest to prevail. What have we to set against this as ordinary people? We are not smarter than Ahriman, nor wiser than Lucifer.

But the Christ stands in the middle. Christ, the Lord of Creation, has handed some control over man and of the earth to Lucifer and Ahriman. They are essential for our development, but they become negative when they extend their territories, which, of course, they do. Then we, the earth, and our culture become ill.

Where do healing forces come from in the human constitution? Where can the Savior work? Where is there free space between Lucifer and Ahriman? I will mention two examples. We need to look for a place where perception and will are equally present—perception that can surrender itself and a fiery will that is ready to serve. The organ Rudolf Steiner speaks about in such terms is the heart. Through study of the heart we can become acquainted with the healing power of Christ.

The second example is revealed when we look to the baby's room. The newborn has balance of surrendering perception and elementary, vital will power. The young child is one-and-all perception and one-and-all will. Is this the reason that the holy silence in the baby's room and the sight of an infant in its cradle appeal so much to us and open our hearts? As the personality of the child emerges, the "sacredness" is lost. But the first three years of childhood are under Christ's rule.

Therapy
My final remarks will be about therapy. Education is a healing process. There are three possible avenues through which therapeutic healing can come: first is our own inner development, second the child's environment, and third the inner therapist within the child. The most beautiful lectures of Rudolf Steiner ever held in this context are the "Bridge Lec-

tures," given on December 17–19 in 1920. Here he tells how the human being can develop toward freedom and love. Our thinking is usually completely directed by what the senses provide to us as the image of reality. We are not free in these images. But there is a way to become freer in our thinking. How? We need to study *The Philosophy of Freedom* and *Across the Boundaries of Natural Science*. This way is a long one, and not everyone will take it up.

Another route is to think about something that you yourself have decided upon, to contemplate something, for one minute a day to begin with. This can be a child you are having difficulties with. Do not take the whole child but just one detail—for example the ear. The next day you can check to see if you have remembered the ear properly. You can adjust your image and perhaps expand your contemplation time to two minutes. There are many books written about how to do this exercise. The point is that rather than letting chance determine what you think about, you decide upon it for yourself. You will find that freedom of thought is not an abstract, distant goal but something that you can get a hold of.

Love is a big word, a worn-out word. Rudolf Steiner uses it in a very practical way. Love means to act in accordance with the situation, to move it forward, and create something new, a right environment. Through recapitulation at the end of the day when we reflect over the day's events, we can see where there has been love and where not. Only in retrospect can we see whether we have helped a situation move forward.

When we think of the environment around little children, we know that it is very important that the true, the beautiful, and the good surround the child. These need to be present in the people around the child as well. It is of utmost importance that children become aware that fairness does not mean that everyone gets the same, but that everyone gets what is right for him or her. They need also to become aware that wisdom deserves a place in its own right, next to intelligence.

The child has three inner therapists working within: play, imagination, and the ability to articulate. It is also true that imitation, reverence, and rhythmic routine are also important helpers in shaping the personality, physically, mentally, and spiritually. But the other three are the innate therapists each child carries within.

In play children shape reality to their will and enter a space in which good and evil, the skillful and clumsy can be present as seems appropriate in the moment. Children who have learned to play cannot be played on so easily later in life.

Imagination has to do with creativity. Fancy things, made-up things, have nothing to do with creativity. Imagination comes from a deep, archetypal source and is connected to the wellspring of art. In play children learn to create and fill their own space.

One of the reasons it is so heartening when children begin to speak is that speaking includes them in a language community. They come under the aegis of the genius of language. This puts children in the common supporting ether stream of the people surrounding them. Of course, language also uses concepts: you can use language to explain what you want to say. But this is not the important point here. Giving words to one's experience and impressions is a powerful tool against the loneliness that children feel when they start to say "I" to themselves. Learning to articulate one's experience lifts the isolation of the I in the physical body.

At this lecture's end, we can look back to where we began. We were so well prepared with our plans and then everything turned out differently than we had expected. Do you know how we got here? How did we manage it?

A concluding photo again showed the island from which we began, but the view is out toward the beach and sea. The dunes have been formed in rhythmic patterns and protect the island from unpredictable moods and power of the sea.

Working with Accelerated and Delayed Development in Early Childhood Education
~ **Dr. Renate Long-Breipohl, Australia**

Introduction
The theme suggested to me for this lecture was that of hindrances to the incarnation of the I. Out of the many possible hindrances I chose to focus mainly on two: on delay with respect to the development of movement, and on acceleration with respect to the development of speech and thinking. These are the two most common challenges for the incarnation of the I in children today. I am well aware that I am speaking out of my experiences with children in an affluent country where children are endangered not by hunger, but by obesity and related conditions, and by overstimulation of the senses. However, I am confident that what is presented here will be relevant, with modification, for children in a wide range of circumstances.

I would like to start with the memory of nine children, who were in my kindergarten in my last year as a practicing kindergarten teacher. Among the twenty-four children of my group, these nine were the ones who did not engage fully in play, but stayed on the fringe. There seemed to be nothing in the room that specifically drew their attention. Their play remained superficial and they were easily distracted by what others were doing.

But one morning towards the end of the school year these nine children did play. They built a boat from chairs and ropes, dressed up (except one) and traveled together in this boat, which was totally overcrowded.

Amazingly this did not unsettle the play. This was so special that I was tempted to take a photo of their play. As soon as I quietly fetched my camera, the play stopped and within seconds they all had placed themselves in position for the photo. I realized that I had disturbed them, but I was also thankful for the opportunity to take the photo, because in the following years this photo became the reminder for me to strive for a deeper understanding of those children who can't enter into play easily and who are not drawn naturally to what the kindergarten has to offer.

There was Thomas[1] standing very upright in the center, dressed with a blue cloak, eyes directed downwards, mouth firmly closed. When he came at the beginning of the year, he wore a fashionable black and white outfit with sunglasses and had spiky gelled hair. Soon it became obvious that he was a very gentle child, with the soft facial features of a much younger child. The spiky hair disappeared and made way for his natural curls. He was quiet and not very active but one day I got to hear his beautiful singing voice and got a glimpse of his musicality. He was a child strong enough to make his mother buy him "real toys," as he said, not the teddy bears he had at home, but the ones we had in kindergarten.

Thomas seemed to be comfortable in the kindergarten environment. However, when he turned six, his parents enrolled him in another private school. At the age of 18 he was already an accomplished pianist. Even though Thomas experienced very little of Steiner education, the time in the kindergarten may have helped him to find his own way into life.

There was Michael, five years old, with a serious look on his face. He was a quiet child, who did not seem to have any specific interest in the daily happenings of the kindergarten. He was alternately withdrawn and then all over the place. He was very attached to his mother and would often stand at the window looking towards the path on which he had seen her leave. He would have liked to be with her, but the mother was so involved in her own life that the child did not get enough attention. Michael did not cry, but there was no joy in him. His sensitivity showed in his skin: he had eczema in the back of the knees and on the legs.

A few years ago I met Michael again. He had grown into a fine, quiet and friendly young man. I talked to him for a little while and then I remarked that in kindergarten he did miss his mother a lot. He nodded, smiled and said, "Yes, I can remember that." It sounded like speaking

---

[1] All names of children have been changed.

about a wound that had healed. Michael, who was feeling insecure and overburdened when he was in kindergarten, found content and stability within himself later, but he remained what he always was: a quiet, gentle person.

There was Tobias, five years old and an only child. The grandparents and the mother were high school teachers. During his time in kindergarten his home environment remained the strongest influence in his life. Tobias was a tall boy, thin, with a large round skull. His gaze was serious, his verbal abilities developed beyond his age, his vocabulary extended.

He was not playing much, but observing other children a lot. One day he came to invite me to watch his puppet show. He led me to a small table which was covered with a cloth but clearly revealed that there was nothing arranged under the cloth. He went behind the table, took off the cloth and stood there saying nothing. "Where is your puppet show," I asked. He answered, "It is imagination."

Tobias never got into the realm of imaginative play in the kindergarten, but he knew that imagination was a word indicating something one cannot see. Tobias stayed for the kindergarten year and then left the school. I don't know how his life story continued.

All three children had no major constitutional hindrances to overcome, but the impact of their life situations was strong. All three had never fully experienced the realm of imaginative play, but they revealed already something of the person they were to become.

The stories of the first two children can lead one to intuit the driving force of development, the incarnating I, working through hindrances placed in the path by inner or outer circumstances. However, Steiner's remark is very true when he says that the I cannot be perceived out of one moment in time.[2] It needs a progression of years. This became clear to me through those children whose paths I could follow into young adulthood.

After pointing to the all-important influence of the individuality on the incarnation process, we will look now more closely at some of the difficulties arising on this path of incarnation.

---

2 Rudolf Steiner, *Education as a Social Problem* (NY: Anthroposophic Press, 1984), p. 76.

Delay in movement development

First, one needs to be careful with the label "delay" and acknowledge that there is a wide range of individual developmental patterns as documented through the research studies of the pediatrician Remo Largo and others.[3]

Second, one needs to acknowledge the significant research which has been done with respect to the development of movement in the first year of life and the role of the primitive reflex patterns.[4] Developmental difficulties may be caused by such primitive reflexes, if they are not integrated at the right time. Reflex integration usually starts in the early months but may not.[5] Primitive reflex patterns may be retained beyond early childhood into the primary school years. Even if these reflexes outwardly disappear, they may remain dormant and may be re-activated under certain circumstances such as stress.

I would like to draw attention to two groups of primitive reflexes. The first group is comprised of the three "fear" reflexes (Fear Paralysis Reflex, Moro Reflex and Withdrawal Reflex), in which fear reactions cause a gesture of freezing. Retention of these reflexes becomes visible in children later in physical activity such as running, ball games, or jumping, but also in the social realm and academic learning.

The second group is made up of the tonic reflexes, which determine the position of parts of the body to each other and regulate the muscle tone.

Let's look at a seven-month-old child. This child was born with constriction in turning her head to one side. The condition was discovered at three weeks after birth and then watched for another month. Through therapy in the following two months the constriction could be alleviated, but the development of movement was delayed. At seven months the TLR backwards, the overstretching of the neck backwards together with

---

[3] See Remo Largo, *Kinderjahre* (Munich, 2000), especially Part I: *Vielfalt und Individualität* (Variety and Individuality).

[4] Sally Goddard Blythe of INPP (Institute of Neuro-Physiological Psychology) in Chester, UK, presented a conference session on April 2, 2012, to describe difficulties children encounter in development when they display retained primitive reflexes that should normally have disappeared during the first year of life.

[5] Reflexes and other approaches are discussed in the article "Movement with Soul," published originally in the UK journal, *Kindling*, and also reprinted in two parts in the WECAN newsletter, *Gateways* (issues 60 and 61, 2011).

arching of the whole body, was clearly visible.[6] The child had previously attempted to turn from back to prone, but because of the arching (TLR), the child could not get enough momentum to roll over.

Between the seventh and ninth month while lying on her tummy, the child frequently went into the "flying bird" gesture (Landau reflex),[7] moving arms and legs as if in flight over extended periods of time, ending each period of flying with vigorously and suddenly putting arms and hands to the front and supporting her lower body in the pelvic and leg area. Then the baby would go back into the Landau position. After several practices the baby would lean her head and upper body sideways and would at some point tip over with hip and legs following. Then the child would lie on her back and rest. When turned back on her tummy, she would start again with the same movement sequence.

After six weeks of practicing she had learned to roll over but there was no visible progress with respect to crawling or sitting. One day, lying in prone position with arms forward, the child supported herself with hands and feet only, having lifted the rest of the body off the ground into a kind of bear walk position. Soon after this she began to bend her knees and succeeded in pulling them under her belly while keeping arms and head up. Now it did not take long at all and the child started crawling. By ten months she was a fast crawler with strong rhythmical movement. She walked shortly before twelve months, but she continued crawling when she wanted to go somewhere fast.

Landau is a transitional reflex from primitive to postural reflexes.[8] Practicing this reflex was this baby's way of building the bridge into getting development moving again. Once she began to crawl, her development moved very quickly. This gives us a picture that there is an inner power at work in the child that wants to move forward in development.

Whether this child will have long-term retained reflexes is an open question. But we saw that she used the reflex to move forward in devel-

---

6 The TLR is one of the tonic reflexes. A description can be found in Sally Goddard Blythe's books *The Well Balanced Child* and *Reflexes, Learning and Behavior* (see note 8).

7 In this position the baby will elevate head, torso, and arms and extended legs off the floor, pivoting on the tummy. The Landau reflex occurs in babies three to twelve months of age.

8 Primitive and postural reflexes are explained in Sally Goddard Blythe, *Reflexes, Learning and Behavior* (Eugene, Oregon: Fern Ridge Press, 2002).

opment. Reflexes can reappear unexpectedly, and hers may do so. But for now she is on a good path. This is an encouraging example. It shows that there is no one way to come into uprightness, but very individual ways to achieve development. It is helpful to look at developmental biographies and progression of the individual child rather than see milestones at certain times.

Hindrances cannot always be worked out by the child himself. Sometimes extra developmental support may be needed. Today research on reflex integration is done in many countries and therapeutic support is available in many places.[9] However, as early childhood educators we should not forget that the development of movement is an activity of the child's soul-spiritual being and that the first three years are guided by spiritual beings who support the eternal individuality of the child in taking hold of the body in the way that is necessary for this particular incarnation. This places a great responsibility on the educator with respect to whether and how extra therapeutic intervention is used.

We should also not forget that our practice in the Steiner kindergartens in general can help to prevent and ease developmental difficulties and can be regarded to some extent as therapy. In making a kindergarten a place of peace and quiet, avoiding stress on children and allowing time and plenty of opportunity for free movement and play, we are creating conditions which promote balance and health in young children.

In our practice we often meet the young child at a point when she may have lived with retained reflexes already for a while and may have developed a corresponding soul habit. Let us look at five-year-old Kate. She has a large, heavy body and is often taken to be older. She is in good health. She has a round head, a large forehead and ears set down low. She has a curve in her back with a protruding tummy.

Her shoulders slouch. Often she has shuffling feet and runs on her tiptoes. In general she moves slowly and cautiously. She jumps heavily and avoids skipping. She is apprehensive about climbing rocks in the

---

[9] For Germany and Austria I would like to mention "Rota Therapy" and the book by Doris Bartel and Sabine Kocher: *Der gesunde Dreh* (Erbach, 2009). Here individually devised sequences of rotational movement exercises are used in order to stimulate balance and normalize the muscle tone, both of which create the condition for overcoming retained reflexes. The effectiveness of working with rotational movements while avoiding movements which trigger reflexes, is documented by case studies only at this stage. An introduction is available on www.rota-therapie.de

playground, but will practice. She is hesitant in using her hands. Only recently has she begun to use a knife and needs help to do so.

From this brief description it is obvious that the physical condition of this child is different from the one of the child just considered. Kate's movement development is slowed down by her low muscle tone, not by too much tension as was the case with the baby.

As Kate is already five, we see something of her speech development as well. She has a good vocabulary and a good ability to memorize stories, which she needs to hear only once in order to retell them. But she will retell the same story again and again. She will also repeat some sentences again and again. She appears to be unaware of what others are saying, as she talks over other children without waiting until they have finished. She tells about herself. She enjoys stories and creates her own in play. She plays intensely, often on her own.

In this girl the delay in the development of movement of legs and hands comes together with a weakness in the perception of social situations and in the ability for communication with others. One can observe here what Steiner indicates in general, namely that the experience of freedom through the sense of movement and the development of social abilities are related.

There is a complex situation of developmental issues in which the soul plays a part as well as the physical body. We have some indications from Rudolf Steiner that may help us to understand the situation.

Rudolf Steiner states that in the lower body the I in conjunction with the will provides the "fire" behind movement: the currents and forces working in the metabolic-limb system start from the I-organization and then flow through the astral, etheric and physical body. In the other pole of the physical body, the sense system, the I provides the intention which stimulates the wish to see and hear what others are doing and saying.[10] With Kate it may be the case that the I is not active enough, both in the metabolic-limb system and the sensory system.

Rudolf Steiner describes the "fantasy rich" child in whom the soul-spirit is not active enough in the lower body, the movement system, and who in consequence is also slow in moving in thoughts, with a tendency to

---

[10] Rudolf Steiner, lecture of February 11, 1923, *The Invisible Man Within Us: The Pathology Underlying Therapy* (Spring Valley, NY: Mercury Press).

repetitiveness. From this picture one can derive indications for developmental support.

As there is some progress in movement development, one could try to encourage free movement first, mainly outdoors by providing opportunities for a variety of movements: skipping, hopping, jumping, climbing, balancing, running, rolling. The work in the morning circle and moving together with a group may be too difficult for Kate at this stage and may have to wait until she is more confident within her body.

With respect to the soul issues, which manifest in the social realm, one could help the development of the dexterity of the hands by supporting playful joyous movements through hand gesture games and finger games in order to invite the child to engage with her feelings. Karl König has linked the refinement of the movements of the hands to the child developing a feeling relationship and interest in the world around.[11] Giving care and attention to the hands may help the child to become more perceptive to her social surroundings and to the other children. It may also help her to become more flexible and agile in her thinking and help with the tendency of fixation in her memory.

With respect to the tendency toward fixation, Steiner points to the importance of music for children who are lacking fluidity in their entire being. Music is a great integrator and a blessing for children who are not moving inwardly enough. The musical element of melody stimulates feeling, and rhythm harmonizes and balances inner and outer movement. Thus music is nourishment for the soul and the body.

Music is an integral part of our work in early childhood, and especially healing when we surround the children with the lightness and gentleness of sound in the mood of the fifth. The experience of music in the mood of the fifth, its liveliness and openness towards the periphery can become a vehicle for the I and the astral body in pervading and enlivening the whole child. Here are tremendous tasks for the early childhood educator, because up to this day the mood of the fifth is not given the chance to play the therapeutic role it could have for young children.[12]

---

11 Karl König, *Being Human* (NY: Anthroposophic Press, 1989).

12 The role of music in general in alleviating developmental delay is described by Sally Goddard Blythe in *The Well Balanced Child*, where she refers to what music meant to her son who faced developmental difficulties. Being an older child already, what helped him was the daily practice of singing as a chorister.

Young children with accelerated development
We turn now to what I see as the biggest hindrance for children today, especially in affluent societies: overstimulation and high performance demands causing accelerated development of the speech and the intellect in young children.

We are looking at the environmental conditions which act adversely on the harmonious joining of the soul-spirit with the physical-etheric body in incarnation and on the emergence of a healthy consciousness of self. We are looking at issues such as the push within the education system for early intellectual performance, and the introduction of modern technology into the lives of young children.

Already in his time Steiner could see the acceleration of intellectual development in children. The individuality, whose presence is felt in the human being through life and who provides the inner experience of self, becomes burdened with sensory overload from the world around at an early age. The children assimilate these influences already early in life and therefore appear much older than they are. Steiner states that there used to be a big difference between the first and the second seven-year periods. He says: "Nowadays children are so very clever... there is little difference between the first and the second seven years. Special methods of education will have to be devised in order to cope with these children. They are as clever as grown-ups and everyone seems equally clever, whatever his age."[13]

This is the most widespread phenomenon of acceleration today. Not only the highly gifted, the exceptional child is affected, but children across the board. This development is a consequence of the nearly exclusive occupation of human thinking with the material world and of the immense importance which is given to information gathering, analyzing, expressing opinions and making judgments. Young children, being imitators, often just repeat information and opinions presented by adults. Children who speak cleverly have been given lots of informative and explanatory input by adults previously and have been encouraged to express opinions and to make decisions from early on.

Childhood was once the time for stories, nursery rhymes, children's songs, time to bring language and meaning to the child musically—not intellec-

---

[13] Rudolf Steiner, *True and False Paths in Spiritual Investigation* (London: 1985, third edition) p. 43.

tually, but through the rhythms and tones of verses and songs. The feeling element of language was important, not the processing of content.

Today many children have a good ability to process information and identify objects already at an early age. An example is an eighteen-month-old boy standing at a coffee table with flash cards. The child was asked to point to the card that showed the house, and so on. The child did perform the task asked of him correctly, but he could not stand at the table independently; he had to hold on to the table to keep his balance.

There was no joy for this child in performing what the adult wanted him to do. At this time of his life he should have been consolidating his upright standing and his walking, not his thinking. However, the common knowledge that the time before the age of three is most effective for accelerating intellectual development has given rise to many early learning programs. Because of their splendid memory children learn quickly how to use words and some concepts correctly, identify representations of objects, name characters from books, recall details of the content, but this does not develop deeper aspects of the child's thinking, and also does not develop feeling and will. Thus children seem to be clever beyond their age, but they are not. While there is acceleration in the intellectual development, there is no corresponding acceleration in the soul. Here the child still follows the seven-year periods of soul development.

An example is a very clever little fellow in my kindergarten, who had something to say about everything. For his fifth birthday celebration in the kindergarten I chose the story about an angel bringing the child down the rainbow bridge to his parents. When the story was finished, the child said in amazement: "Is that how it was?" He felt the truth of this picture in his soul. Intellectually he had absorbed other information about birth given by his parents. But even in such an intellectually awake child, the soul resonated with this picture of birth.

Steiner has warned that putting demands of early intellectual performance on the growth forces of the young child before the age of seven will cause stress and lead to the etheric sheath around the child becoming "thin." Its life-giving quality will be damaged. The strain shows in the children as nervousness, loss of focused interest in their surroundings, and restless behavior. These are signs of overload of the soul, not the intellect.

I would like come back to Tobias, the child with early intellectual devopment mentioned at the beginning. His soul did not take part in his intellectual advancement; the joyless look in his eyes and his inability to play showed that his soul was undernourished.

Tobias also spoke with a monotonous voice. When he was stressed his voice became shrill and high-pitched and he gasped for air between the words, a sign that breathing and feeling were cramped and not able to flow out unhindered.

Tobias was not only an intellectually awake child, but also an anxious child. This was physically expressed in his awkward running style, with the leaning backwards of his upper body while running, which made him a very slow runner.

Children such as Tobias react to overstimulation with anxiety, not with fear of something specific, but with fear as a general soul condition. I regard this fearfulness as a significant hindrance in the incarnation process. It is visible in many children today. It adversely affects not only play, but also sleeping and eating. Sometimes we see this fear expressed as a physical gesture when the child flexes his hands closed, almost as a reflexive action.

Six-year-old Benjamin is such a generally fearful child. He is tall, thin, has a long narrow face, wide-open fearful looking eyes, a monotonous voice, and tense movements. He is a very picky eater and constantly on the watch for what is going on around him. Hopefully the warmth of his new teacher and the routines and rhythms of the kindergarten will help him feel more secure. He is just starting to smile occasionally and to play a little.

Steiner spoke about those children whose astral body and I are too much drawn out into the environment.[14] This is very relevant not only for children who are fearful, but also for those who live with so much enticement and distraction around them that they lose their secure base. Steiner states that children become inwardly oversensitive and sore and in consequence they are prone to actions that cover up this discomfort with overactive behavior. The soul fear which seems to become more prominent in young children goes along with early I consciousness. Saying "I" to themselves used to be the sign that the child had reached an inner threshold and a new developmental stage. Today children say I often as early as at eighteen months, not at three years.

---

14 Rudolf Steiner, *Education for Special Needs*, Lecture 4.

Steiner describes the I consciousness at age three as follows: The I pictures to himself mental images in saying "I feel,"" I suffer" and so on; this is linked to the concept I which is noticed by the child around age three.[15] But Steiner also mentions the saying "I" from the age of eighteen months onwards and attributes this saying I to imitation, at this stage without the deeper aspect of self as different from others.

One hears young children say "I want this, I want that." These are expressions of desire which may be misunderstood as arising from being conscious of oneself as an I. This "I want" is always linked to environmental influences, to the immense role which desire and its satisfaction plays in modern life. It is also linked to children being frequently asked about their wishes and asked to make choices. This early saying "I" is not due to acceleration in the emergence of consciousness of self, but rather arises from early intellectual alertness and needs to be seen in connection with the role of consumerism and advertising in society.

Pedagogical practice in the face of delay and acceleration
In our pedagogical practice we must reflect on what is essential and what is less important. There is one essential for early childhood educators, which surmounts all others: to understand human nature and how it specifically appears in young children. Only based on such understanding can we become helpers of the I in the incarnation process to find the right support for a harmonious development and the establishment of balance between the three centers of activity in the child's body, the nerve-sense system, the rhythmical system and the metabolic-limb system.[16] This holds true for all children.

However, the I meets different conditions and incarnation occurs slightly differently in each child. We need to develop the faculty of intuition in order to understand what is specific about the incarnation process of a particular child.[17]

---

15 Rudolf Steiner, *Life Between Death and Rebirth* (NY: Anthroposophic Press, 1968), p. 34.

16 Rudolf Steiner, in a lecture of August 18, 1922: "All true teaching and pedagogy must be based on the knowledge of the human nature." *The Spiritual Ground of Education* (NY: Anthroposophic Press, 2004), p. 35.

17 In order to develop this intuition Steiner has given us pictures of the incarnation process: the picture of child development, the picture of the connection of the physical-etheric and the soul-spiritual aspect in the child's temperament and the constitutional pictures. A summary of the constitutional types can be found in Michaela Glöckler, *Education as Preventive Medicine* (CA: Rudolf Steiner College Press, 2002), pp. 76-86. Previously published in German as *Gesundheit und Schule* (Verlag am Goetheanum, 1998).

The seven-month-old baby Kate, Thomas, and Michael tell the teacher something important about incarnation: A lot is worked out by the child himself according to his destiny, sometimes only over years. Yet we need to understand that we, in whatever we do, become part of the child's destiny. Where we see problems, we need to be cautious and allow a reasonable time to observe. We must ask ourselves where we see progress, where not. We need to keep in touch with others, doctors, colleagues, therapists to sense what will be appropriate restraint or support for the child.

Thus as teachers we work on two levels: First, we work with what all young children need. We have our Waldorf Early Childhood Curriculum with essentials such as creating a calm and peaceful environment, providing examples worthy of imitation, creating rhythmical flow in the life of the kindergarten, facilitating self-directed play, and guiding activities such as the circle, storytelling, music.[18] Through this we create life experiences that are conducive to health also for children with delayed or accelerated development.

Many children are thriving on what we are able to offer: the mood of the kindergarten, the images, the activities, the working adult, the togetherness in the group.

But there are children who are not, such as those described at the beginning. Therefore, secondly we have the task of making adjustments with respect to those children.

Steiner has given us the task of removing hindrances so that the child's spirit may enter with full freedom into life.[19] As a teacher today one needs to remind oneself that incarnation has become more difficult in our time and that therefore we meet more difficult children. Steiner admonishes us not to experience this as a tragedy, but to see every difficult child as a gift by the spiritual world and a "manifestation of the highest.

---

18 In her lecture at the International Waldorf/Steiner Early Childhood Conference in 2005 Michaela Glöckler said, "The theme we have touched here, that of relationship–play–development, really is a threefold constellation which can be a lodestar for us, to such a degree that we can only say, from a medical point of view: Dear Waldorf Movement, dear Waldorf Kindergarten Movement, have faith that this health concept, this concept of development which we are working with, will prove itself more and more in the coming years. People will discover by and by that this is a concept that is in tune with child development." *Playing, Learning, Meeting the Other* (Spring Valley, NY: WECAN, 2007), p. 30.

19 *The Spiritual Ground of Education*, p. 56.

We must live through this feeling of tragedy, because this feeling will help us perceive, how something bad can also be something divine."[20]

Reflecting on my experiences, I would like to suggest adjustments to three essential parts of our work: to forming relationships with children, to working with imitation and example, and to guiding play.

Regarding our relationships with children, all we can achieve is based upon how much we can develop ourselves. As Rudolf Steiner states: "We educate children that are cleverer than we are. We can, because we educate through the will and the heart up to that stage of perfection which we have achieved."[21]

The children whom I found challenging taught me the following:

- Patience, because the I may not be visible over long periods of time;

- Acceptance of destiny: some children's lives will take a different direction than I may have wished;

- Letting go of the illusion that one will always be able to find a cure for difficulties in the development and lives of children;

- Realizing that those children who stay on the fringe of the life and the activities in the kindergarten do rely even more than other children on the closeness and warmth of the one-to-one relationship between teacher and child;

- Developing the inner gesture of walking side by side with the child, that is, of carrying the child's challenges with him and thus alleviating the child's burden.

In a world that is widely materialistic and cold, we can strive to embrace children, who suffer from the conditions of modern life, with the warmth of our inner being; we can hold children in our thoughts and accept that some challenges, which these children face, will not resolve.

The heavy body of Kate will remain, but the child may learn to live in it more comfortably. The child with accelerated intellectual development will always tend toward thinking and have a tendency to be anxious, but may experience more joy and become more relaxed in daily life.

---

20 *The Spiritual Ground of Education*, p. 55.

21 Rudolf Steiner, *The Foundations of Human Experience*, Lecture 10.

One must also realize that symptoms may go away in one place but reappear somewhere else. Physical symptoms may go, but more permanent soul reactions may form instead. This is especially the case with anxiety and fear. The child who is shy may remain shy. Such soul conditions are part of our karma and thus part of who we are.

As the teacher practices this walking side by side with the hypersensitive and anxious child, the role of the teacher changes. She is not only the "group ego" and guardian of the place, but she uses her own ego forces to strengthen the ego of a child in need who is looking for such support.

Extending imitation
Imitation is a gift of the spiritual world, a helper with incarnation. Steiner speaks about the ability of all young children to merge inwardly with another human being as originating in spiritual existence before birth. That this ability develops on earth in early childhood is the condition for becoming a free human being later in life. Also he states that "the benefit for a child is all the greater, the more he is able to live not in his own soul but in those within his environment."[22] Imitation is the practice of this ability to live within the other human being. In general as teachers we set an example by uniting consciously with what we are doing, so that sense impressions are created which "ripple through the organs of the child" in a harmonious way and therefore are health giving.[23]

Steiner warns that "if we do not know that the physical body must become an imitator in the right way, we shall merely implant animal instincts in this body."[24] We can observe in children today the tendency to imitate the subhuman. It is reinforced by many modern children's books depicting a subhuman world through caricatured invented creatures or exaggerations of animal features. Many children today have not experienced enough actions which are worthy of imitation and they may have ceased imitating at all at an early age. Therefore working with imitation and example may need to be therapeutically extended for those children who are not imitators naturally, and who are anxious and self-conscious about their own performance.

---

22 Rudolf Steiner, *Education as a Social Problem*.

23 Rudolf Steiner, *The Education of the Child in the Light of Anthroposophy*.

24 *Education as a Social Problem*.

A child, who is just about to do something, asks the adult: "You do that too?" It is the question of a fearful, insecure child. It does not mean "Show me," it means "Let us do it together, then I feel safe." This request may occur in play inside or outside as well as while sitting at the table drawing or doing crafts. "You do that too?" It is the request for a more intimate connection.

Normally we trust that the child will feel connected and will imitate naturally. As imitation arises from deep within the child, one would not want to influence the process directly. With some children today this may not be the case. We are then inclined to speak of weakness in imitation.

There is a very interesting example which Steiner gives in *Education for Special Needs*. There he speaks about children who tend towards anxiety and even depression. He speaks about the fear in the child of not being able to do something. Today this fear is quite widespread already in three-year-olds. Steiner suggests doing an activity with the child, not for the child. "Say, you get the child to paint. You do not paint yourself; but you sit down by him and move your paint brush, accompanying with your brush each movement he makes with his... Thus, with love in your heart, you do with him what he has to do; the fact that you are there beside him in this way—he will feel it like a gentle caress in his soul. Right down to such intimate details are we able to find what we have to do through careful observation of the situation."[25]

What is important is the "doing with the child" so that this doing-with has the quality of a gentle caress. This is not for the whole group or every child; this is for the children who are anxious and have lost the trust in themselves and their own ability. We have many of those "I can't do it" children in our kindergartens. The remedy could be a modified kind of imitation, in which the child leads as much as the adult within a warm, caring situation.

If the teacher paints with a small group of children, she may sit next to a child in need of "doing it with you" and then the teacher will paint out of an inner feeling of togetherness with the child, and out of the fine observation of what is expressed in the child's brushstrokes and colors. This can be applied to baking as well, to kneading together, modelling

---

25 Rudolf Steiner, *Education for Special Needs*, Lecture 4.

together, and possibly to crafts, and in some instances to play. It is not copying the child. It is an extension of working with imitation and example aimed at creating an extra protective, supportive sheath for a specific child, a sheath made of empathy.

Extending the practice of guiding play
Healthy play develops when the child initiates and leads his own play without adult intervention. We would like to see children immersed and relaxed in these timeless moments of play, able to bring forth through their will what lives within them. Inner joy and peace can arise out of such play for those children who are able to enter into it deeply.

We observe what interests the child, whether the child can play out of inner peace and for how long he can be absorbed in such play. Often children with early intellectual development find it difficult to play intensely. Their play activity remains on the surface, as they roam about and look at what others are doing.

In some instances it may be necessary to extend one's tolerance of what is "nice" or "good" play. Then one may hold back from redirecting and allow play to continue so that children can play out something they need to process. The following example involved two children who were playing a fighting game that overwhelmed them. For me it is an example of children playing out fear, and it is important to allow such play to happen, even if it is not harmonious, calm and pleasant.

The children are three to five years old in a home-based care situation with five children present per day. I think the following play was possible because it was happening within a small-group situation and did not disturb other children.

From the back room near the bathroom, noises can be heard as if rockets were launched. Then one boy comes into the main play room dragging a large blue cloth behind him. He throws himself on the floor. "I am dead," he says. The other boy comes out of the back room with a large red cloth, waving it at the boy: "I make you come alive again." The boy gets up and both children start a fight between the blue and the red cloth, waving them vigorously. Fire and water are battling; the water wants to extinguish the fire. Then the play changes: both boys fight now together against a monster. They cannot kill it, only escape from it. Now "bad ones" are after both of them. The boys run across the room into the doll's house. "Here we are safe, let's eat." Some wooden "apples" and "eggs" go to their mouths. Chairs are moved to block the entrance. The monster is coming. No escape. They rush to the gate of their house to fight it, then move to the back of the house to make a better weapon: a rod with a flat piece of wood stuck at one end. They call it "sword." Both are holding their swords, gesticulating wildly. Now they become pirates, the house is their ship. At this moment the teacher walks up, having seen the children gesticulate with sticks. She says: "I give you a nice long string, so you can have a good fishing rod." They decline. "We are pirates," they say. They want a flag. The teacher comes back with two pieces of cloth, ties these to their sticks. They are wildly swung. Teacher: "Gentle hands." The boys disappear to the back room. Noises of rockets are heard again. The teacher goes to get a ball and the children are asked to come outside for a ball game.[26]

One may be in two minds about this play. The teacher certainly was, because she tried to divert the play into a fishing game and then finished the play situation on her terms. Should these children have the opportunity to play in this way? Part of the play is possibly influenced by TV, part of it is determined by their own fears and their own fantasies. The play process was dynamic, and there was nothing vicious in this play; both children played together and played intensely.

I suggest that there is a place for such play in Steiner early childhood education, that this kind of play is part of being a child today. It does make a difference if children have the opportunity to play out their fears. Over time the transformation which happens through play can bring healing and peace to those children.

As a contrasting and yet somehow similar anecdote I would also like to relate a puppet story which was invented, told and performed in my kindergarten by six-year-old Rose.

The story began with a number of people/puppets entering a forest, eating berries from a bush and falling asleep. A huntsman came and killed them in their sleep. Then the king went into the forest accompanied by a little girl. He wanted to know what was going on. He ate some berries and fell asleep. Then came the huntsman and killed the king. The girl went to the castle to tell the queen what had happened. Then the girl led the prince into the forest and the prince found the king. At this moment Rose took the crown off the king and put it on the head of the prince.

---

26 This example is taken from Renate Long-Breipohl, *Supporting Self-Directed Play in Steiner/Waldorf Early Childhood Education* (Spring Valley, NY: WECAN, 2010).

Then the prince went back to the castle with the girl and the prince married the queen and they lived happily ever after.

The girl who told this story was one of the most peaceful and social children in the kindergarten. During her puppet show she was totally engrossed in the story and told it with rosy cheeks and a smile on her face. This story was not "pretty or nice." From the perspective of modern consciousness one could call it dark. It reminded one of themes of ancient mythology, it did not contain emotions in the way we know it; just the facts were told. There was no judgment about good and bad, as was the case in the play of the two boys. All these are indications that one has to regard this story as arising within the child from a different time and a different consciousness than we experience today, and the consciousness from which the play of the two boys originated. They played out fears related to the modern world. The story and the way Rose told it mirrored the dream consciousness, which according to Steiner connects young children to the ancient times of mythological stories. This dream consciousness and the play arising out of it should be given a place in our kindergartens too. Experiencing such play out of dream consciousness will help the children whose accelerated awake thinking does not allow them to access their own dream consciousness in play. Although they will not initiate such play themselves, they will nevertheless benefit from such play happening around them.

Thus the kindergarten can become a place for the past and the present, the dreamers and the thinkers, the experience of difficult aspects of life as well as the good, the true and the beautiful, to the extent that they belong to the life and the being of young children.

Twelve Doorways to the World: The I and the Body in Sensory Experience

~ **Claus-Peter Röh, Switzerland**

Every morning this week in the eurythmy performances we have had a stream of humanity on the stage from Isis to Sophia, from the dawn of humanity to the present.[1] These are inner images we all carry in us when we come into life through the portal of birth. A second stream representing humanity was the big map we saw the other evening when we had artistic presentations from our colleagues from all over the world. For a moment there was a spark of the thought that this is humanity. Only through encountering the other are we each truly whole and a part of humanity.

People who were born in a Christian culture celebrate that tomorrow is the Friday before Easter. And they look toward Easter as the festival of resurrection. We will look later at how a child experiences the passage from Good Friday to Easter. In every religion we will find that something dies from the past so something new can be born. We let go of something old so something new can come.

Last year, after Heinz Zimmermann died, Christof Wiechert highlighted this theme of development and transformation in Heinz's biography. Heinz Zimmermann brought many karmic tasks with him into his

---

1 See note on page 24.

life. Then a point came somewhere in the middle of his life when he experienced himself as free from these tasks and could work for human beings out of inner freedom. Out of this karmic fulfillment, Heinz Zimmermann could work strongly into social life.

Today our theme is the twelve senses, twelve gateways to the world though which we can experience different perspectives. In the question of religion it is also important to look and ask questions from different perspectives. We have many religions around the world with differing views. Yet when there are urgent needs, everyone resounds together as one humanity. Last summer in Oslo when so many young people were killed, thousands of mourners came together and were meeting each other in a very peaceful way. For a moment, the possibility for our human future lit up, which overcomes any narrow world views. A Norwegian Islamic writer, Walid Al-Kubaisi, said: "I am a Muslim. But not only a Muslim Arab. I am a Christian because I have the feeling that truth incarnates itself in man. I am a Jew because I believe that I am an individually chosen one. I am French because I love Voltaire, Norwegian because Wergeland inspires me every day." Goethe was describing the strength to go through death so that we can develop the new with the words, "And so long as you have not attained it, this 'Die and become!', you will only be a gloomy guest on this dark earth." Openness for the future, for the next step of development, is connected to the senses.

Let us observe through the gaze of sense experience a child of three-and-a-half. She is living in what happens in her surroundings in such a way that on an Easter morning walk she perceives the festive atmosphere. How does a child of this age relate to Easter? On Easter morning the family steps into the garden. The child has sensed through imitation that something special is happening. In imitation the child lives wholly through the behavior of the rest of the family. When a rabbit runs slowly along in a neighboring field, she shouts a greeting out of the depths of her heart to this real, live "Easter Rabbit."

The child is full of expectation; this feeling comes from inside herself. Then suddenly the older brother calls that the Easter rabbit has come. A silk cloth is pulled away to reveal a treasure of Easter eggs, and there is a sudden realization, connecting all these impressions. The child calls out, "Thank you for all the Easter eggs!" There is deep stimulation in the soul and the answer comes from inside the child.

We may ask why it is that today, in our kindergartens and in the transition to first grade, we have to strive so hard for the capacity of imitation in the young child. What stands in the way of these forces of healthy development in our time? Rudolf Steiner observed two sides of childhood today. On the one hand the child has a dried-out, fragmented outer appearance, and on the other hand "deep inside is the true human being. This no longer comes to outward expression in the way it did until the fifteenth century. We will have to get more and more used to the thought that, especially in the case of children, the inward human being cannot be fully revealed by the way people present themselves, nor by the way they think and the gestures they make. In many respects these children are something quite different from what comes to outward expression. We even know extreme cases. Children may appear to be the worst of rascals and yet there is so much good in them that they will later be the most valuable of human beings."[2] As educators we have to have a prophetic gift to see this inner I and to work towards it. Think of all the impossible, restless children in our classes, who want to become the true I. For Rudolf Steiner, this development of inner activity is connected with the task of our times; people must find through an inner struggle what is no longer given through natural means, in order to have the possibility of freedom.

Much has been asked of us in this sense through the previous lectures during our conference. Louise deForest encouraged us to be truthful in looking at our daily lives and courageously ask, "Why am I doing what I do?" Michaela Glöckler looked to the I as the point and to the encounters we experience every day in our work as coming from the outside, from the periphery. How do I deal with what comes toward me? And she also spoke of the persona who steps forward. Edmond Schoorel pointed out that the child, and we adults, too, have to newly improvise every day, because things do not turn out as we anticipate; we have to adapt. Renate Long-Breipohl spoke of the attitude with which we meet the individual child. What do we recognize as too early or too late in the child's development? How must I act so that I do not take away the next step of the child's development by intervening or offering help too soon?

Many parents know these difficult questions today. A colleague with three children says of her youngest that she does not understand him. He insists and resists with such power. His forces grow, because he wants to do things according to his own will and in his own time. Then

---

2 GA 177, *The Fall of the Spirits of Darkness*, Lecture 6, October 8, 1917.

she reflects, "I don't understand him, but he is just amazing." She sees what is in him.

A strong future force comes through those children in our families and our schools. A seventh grade teacher is on the way to class, and a little five-year-old boy crosses his path on his way to his own "work." The child calls out, "Good luck today. You will be all right." Many children today bring this positivity with them.

The consideration of how the I, the soul, and the body of the child relate to each other stands before us as a question. Each educator has to confront this same question as an individual as well. Am I too concentrated in myself, too much in my own soul? Am I too one-sidedly turned toward the outside, lost in outer perception? Or do I have clarity in perception? Am I balanced in my judgment? Where am I in harmony? When Rudolf Steiner was speaking in a spiritual context he also was looking with interest at the scientific research of his time. In 1922 in Oxford he stated that if we would have a more subtle, refined physiology, then we would see that in the developing child there is incredible inner activity, more than we can perceive from the outside.

In his book *Lob der Schule*, Joachim Bauer has described the research on the mirror neurons, the mechanism that lives within each of us in the brain and allows the capacity to imitate—to watch and then to act out—that Rudolf Steiner had referred to as "refined physiology." All we see is quietly imitated in the brain of the observer like in a mirror. Dr. Bauer realized that he could show this enormous activity going on in the brain.

The child is wholly sense organ. What does this mean? What happens now in eye, ear, and the sense of touch? How can that take hold of the person from head to toe? Within ourselves we are experiencing what is going on outside of ourselves.

An example of a three-and-a-half- or four-year-old child sitting quietly in the garden in the summer illustrates this. The child is totally absorbed; this is one characteristic of being a sense organ. The child is sitting still, but on his hand a snail is moving very slowly. For hours he watches this play of the feelers coming out, then withdrawing when there is a little fright. The child watches without moving. The whole world is the snail. Then two days later out on a walk while the adults are speaking and not noticing anything to the left or right, suddenly from afar a car approaches fast and loud. Only then do the adults notice that the little child is not with them. Looking back they see the child slowly creeping, crawling on the road. The parents dash to get the child to safety. "What were you doing?" the parents ask. The child replies, "Little snail." The child has become so much the snail of two days before that now he is the snail. What an enormous force of the I, of the self, is engaged to take this in so much. What has taken this in so deeply and brought it again out into life? The I has to do with this activity.

A second example, which will shed light on several levels, comes from when one family visits another with lots of children. Two brothers from the visiting family, six-and-a-half and four years of age, enter into the host children's room. The older brother sees a bow and arrow in the corner. He goes straight toward the bow, looks at it, takes it with the gesture of an expert, places the arrow, and aims at the target. *Bang.* The arrow with the rubber tip hits the target and sticks. Then this child is finished with it and looks for the next thing.

But the four-year-old looks on still in total devotion. The little brother now takes the bow and grabs hold of it by the string rather than the wooden hand-hold, and the bow always twirls round in his hand. He takes the other hand and gets hold. But in his imitation, something is not quite the same. Now as soon as he lets go to grab an arrow, the bow begins to wobble again. Now he stands with the same gesture as his brother, turns toward the target, and sets the arrow. Yet it is obvious that something is still missing. Instead of drawing the bowstring and arrow, he throws the arrow into the right direction.

On the one hand this is imitation. But there is also the question of who is being imitated, not only what. During the night the child makes a choice from a higher point of view of what is imitated and what is not. Not everything is imitated. In the way the boy imitated his brother, we saw that he wanted to do everything his brother did. In the school and in the kindergarten, the children bring this deep wish forth toward their educators. This is the destiny, the karma aspect of imitation, and we then have the question of how we can help our children today to strengthen and foster the will forces of imitation.

Two polarities come into play now when we consider sense experience. Where are the twelve senses with regard to the young person? We have two streams. The one [indicated by a drawing on the board as blue streaming from below upward] is the stream which we bring from the past, from Isis to Sophia, the stream of wisdom. These are the inner images we bring from life before birth. Then through the twelve senses we turn toward the world, toward the future, from which the sense-experiences approach us. [This is indicated on the board as a red counter-stream coming from above downward.]

An example from the past/blue stream can be seen in questions a four-year-old asks. "Mummy, how does God make hair grow?" The parent answers, "It grows like grass." The next question is, "How does God make legs and arms grow?" These are questions coming from the inner stream of wisdom.

Then from the other stream come other questions. A little child is sleeping in the car and is wakened by a loud bang. He wakes with a start, jerks eyes open, and stretches his arms like a marionette moved from outside. But then the child continues to sleep. The I of the child is outside in the surroundings. It perceives what has happened, and reacts in the limbs, but the child goes on sleeping. What happens in the middle realm of the soul? The senses go on the red stream, to the future. Little children intensively take in the environment in their experience and then do something with it. In another example, on a crowded train before a football match, the people are loud and restless; and a five-year-old girl becomes frightened and clutches her mother. But the mother whispers into her ear a story about a king and princess, and the child calms down as she is immersed in the pictures of the story.

Another five-year-old girl is in the airport, standing in a line of about fifty people where everyone is slowly advancing. Because the child is inwardly active in imitation, she copies this gait of the grownups. Then she discovers some puppets moving on a screen and begins to move like them, in complete earnestness and devotion. Here also, the inner will of the girl to imitate is impressively strong.

To summarize, we can recognize that in the middle of the human being, in the soul, two strong streams are encountering each other: the stream of sense-experience, which comes towards us from outside and streams toward the future in the daily perception of the world; and the wisdom-stream from the past, from Isis to Sophia, which we bring within us from before birth.

The sense of touch is the foundation of the twelve senses. Even before birth the mother may notice the movement of the child, the touching within. The birth process itself is fundamentally woven through by the sense of touch. Following this the child is swaddled and held, and soon after that he starts to grasp the fingers of the parent. This sense of touch has immense power. Where is it based? On the one hand, we perceive the world as a reality through the sense of touch. But as this sense brings us to the border between body and world, at the same time it brings an experience of the self in the body. Herein lies the mysterious double aspect of the sense of touch. As we perceive the outside world at the sense-border of the body, at the same time we perceive ourselves as self within the body. Rudolf Steiner, in describing the sense of touch, explained that the important aspect of touch is that the human being experiences himself in his body by finding himself inwardly. This is the double aspect of touching.

To experience this dual aspect we might remember for ourselves an experience from childhood. An example is offered by two brothers living in an old farmhouse with their parents. The parents have gone to a party and the boys are left to put themselves to bed. The older brother asks if the younger is scared. The little one says no. The wind may be shaking the roof tiles, but the little one denies fright. Then the older brother goes to sleep and the little one stays awake. Then the younger one wonders if the parents actually locked the door. He can't sleep unless he is absolutely sure. He walks through the big house in the dark, feeling his way over rough creaking stairways, cold stone floors, warm wooden floors, doorways and thresholds. His hands are touching the banisters, door handles, edges of walls. The more touching and feeling there is, the stronger grows his confidence of "I am I." He gets to the door and finds that the door is locked. There he has an inner feeling of strength. "I know my home. I can do this." Then he returns to bed peaceful and quiet. Touch is deeply connected with I-awareness.

From the perspective of anthroposophy, there is always a higher sense linked with a foundational sense.[3] What we develop in terms of security comes through our organ for touch. Polar opposite to this sense of touch is the ability to perceive the I of the other person. At the borders of the sense of touch, I am experiencing myself as an I from within. The I or ego sense is a sense to experience not myself, but the I of the other being from without. What is the organ for the sense of I? With touch it

---

3 The twelve senses as described by Rudolf Steiner were written on the board. These are divided into the four foundational senses of touch, life, self-movement, and balance; the middle soul senses of smell, taste, sight, and warmth; and the four higher/social/spiritual senses of hearing, word, thought, and the sense to perceive the ego of the other human being. The four foundational and the four higher senses are inter-related, as explained in the rest of this lecture.

is the skin and mucous linings. The organ for the sense of I is the *gestalt* of the human being itself, the human form as a unified whole. For a real ego-meeting, it is often very important to stand or sit really upright in front of the other.

I can perceive you if I can meet you. I have an organ to perceive you as an I. Through intuition I go into the other and perceive both other and self. The sense of the other person's I comes from the outside through the ego sense, and the sense of one's self comes from the inside with the sense of touch. Rudolf Steiner states that this sense is there so we can spiritually extend our sense of touch/I beyond the body.

There is a question about children who do not have self-confidence, children who are anxious. These children can identify more strongly with their own body if we can work with them on the sense of touch. They often respond well to working the earth, soil, clay, and other materials on the way to overcoming fear and gaining self-confidence.

In the morning when waking up, sometimes we can observe the second of the lower senses, which usually stays completely unconscious. But when we notice upon awaking that one place in the body is not right or in order, this sense says immediately, "There it is." This life sense or well-being sense perceives us as a whole human being, and informs us if something is wrong with the life forces or with our health. As educators we try to make it possible for the child to have many moments of feeling harmonious and healthy. What is now the unconscious side of the sense of life? If a child experiences a pain consciously, we immediately put a bandage on it. Unconsciously the I of the human being in the body has the experience through the life sense that it is one organism. I experience myself as a unity, as a wholeness. And this unity, I experience as well-being. If we succeed as parents and educators in helping the children to build up and strengthen this unity, the bodily experience of the life sense transforms itself into the higher ability of sense of thought.

Some months ago, in an educational support conference with a focus on math, those upbuilding steps between sense of life and sense of thought showed themselves with differentiated clarity. The quality of a particular math operation can be grasped by the children in thought only when in the body-experience through the sense of life there is first this experience of inner unity. The experience of the body-unity later becomes the foundation of the experience of mathematical unity.

At the conference it became shockingly clear how many children today have to live afresh through the experiences of the basic senses with tremendous force and help, so that they can again build up an inner ground to serve as a foundation—for the understanding of the different math operations, for instance. This inner ground is not to be thought of as material. Even though the sense of touch in its primary experience engages intensively with the outer sense world of objects, ground, other people, in its mature stage, soul forces are building the confidence and security which then inwardly can carry the process of doing mathematics.

When we ask how we can help children who are not awake to learning, we find that everything concerning numeracy depends upon this feeling oneself as a unity. I first have to experience myself as a unity before my thinking can proceed into mathematical operations. The sense of life and thinking are existentially connected.

In a lecture on September 2, 1916, Rudolf Steiner described how the four foundational or will senses work "from within" as the basis for the development of the higher senses in their perception "from without." In this way, each of the basic senses has a higher sense which corresponds to it:

I-sense	**Thought**	**Word**	**Hearing**
Warmth	Sight	Taste	Smell
Touch	**Life**	**Self-movement**	**Balance**

In this chart, the mighty pedagogical and biographical influence of the twelve senses on the relationship of "I" and body shows itself. The richer the experience of the bodily, foundational senses in early childhood, the more freely and strongly the ego can develop new soul capacities out of this wellspring.

- The confidence-in-life of the touch experience transforms into the ability to perceive the I of the other from without.

- The experience of identity with the unity of the bodily organization in the sense of life becomes the ability to perceive thoughts and further develop them.

- The joy of outer movement can later become the joy of perceiving language out of one's inner self, the ability to move freely in language.

- The sense of balance is connected to the physical organization of the ear, along with the sense of hearing. Both of these senses contain the gesture of completely giving up oneself to the surroundings. You can observe how a child when balancing gives himself completely to the balancing movements.

We know there are children who are very one-sided. They are in the head too early, but they do not have balance in the lower being. They are not fully with their I and haven't really arrived in the body. We have heard of children who are not mobile in their language yet. Some children have no balance between the upper and lower being. Rudolf Steiner focuses on the balance between one and the other. The educator is to see the whole person and find the balance:

> We can already see how necessary it is to pay attention to that state of balance which needs to be established between the luciferic and the ahrimanic forces in the world. This is the most essential and significant thing. Just consider how the human I is involved in the extremes of both sides: here, the I without and, in the sense of touch, the I within. Similarly, the astral body is involved both in thinking, and also, from within, in the life organism. The etheric body is involved here, as long as speech does not occur, but is also involved from within in the sense of movement. And, holding the middle, like the unmoving hypomochlion at the centre of a pair of scales, we have a sphere that is not so involved in the 'I touch — I think — I live — I speak — I move.' The more closely one approaches this center, the more immobile the arm of the scales becomes. To either side, it is deflected. Thus there is a kind of state of balance at the middle.[4]

In conclusion, let's look at the middle senses: warmth, sight, taste and smell. Then we have a complete field of senses before us, which in the experience of the children is especially strongly connected with the middle being, the feeling-perceiving realm. If young children are exhausted after a long hike or a lengthy running game, then the restlessness, tension and exhaustion are transformed completely when the whole group sits in the warm sun and eats the food they brought along, and perhaps watches a flock of birds flying by. After each challenge, before each new step in learning, or just in general in life, it is of essential significance if one succeeds in establishing a constantly new balance between the recognizing senses, which are directed outwards, and the inner experiences of the corresponding will or bodily senses. This power of being able to find the center again was described by Rudolf Steiner in the quotation above.

So it is clear that the twelve senses as gateways to the world from one point of view are very different. In the lower, foundational senses, we

---

4 From GA 170, *The Riddle of Humanity*, Lecture 14, September 2, 1916.

experience ourselves as ego in the body and in the unconsciously-working forces of the world, whereas through the gate of the higher senses, the world can stream into our consciousness. Some gateways are more open from the outside and others from the inside. The middle ones open to both inside and outside.

Why does this concern us so much today? Why can this be a key into understanding the incarnation of the I into the body? We never experience only one sense alone. There are children's games where all the senses resound together as one. When this happens, we are human in a particular way. We are called upon to come to our own inner, active judgment. If I give children lots of sensory stimulation, the child has to make the inner activity to bring it all together. Touch wants to bring its own experience together with what comes from the other senses. Out of our I we have the capacity to bring everything together. If we see a tree outside in white blossom, we do not see the tree with our eye alone. Our eye sees the white of the blossoms; the eye sees colors. But our sense of balance, which works in the depths of perception, says that the tree is really *there* as I am also *here*. From out of the I, the viewer actively connects those planes into a wholeness of perception.

In a nearby kindergarten three children were playing together. It was wonderful to experience how the play transformed from one activity to another. They rode in a big swinging basket together and laughed for joy. Then they ran to the building where a man was sweeping. They swept for a while, went on to digging in the sandbox, and finally returned to the swing. Then a conversation began. The little one said, "We are traveling to the south pole." Then the middle one said, "It is different at the south pole." After a moment of silence, the oldest finally said, "No. At the south pole it is *completely* different."

In essence this hour of play was a choreography of sense-experiences. And who is the choreographer? It is the I of the child, in harmony with the others in play.

I thank you, and hope that in future a similar harmony of working can develop between school teachers and kindergarten teachers.

Biographical Notes

Louise deForest was an early childhood educator for many years. She now dedicates herself to the mentoring and evaluating of teachers and programs and is actively involved with teacher training in the US, Canada, Mexico and Europe. She offers lectures and workshops in many countries and travels widely. She is a board member of WECAN and is one of two North American representatives to the International Association for Steiner/Waldorf Early Childhood Education (IASWECE) Council.

Michaela Glöckler was a practicing pediatrician and school doctor in Germany for ten years. Since Easter of 1988 she has led the Medical Section of the School for Spiritual Science at the Goetheanum in Dornach, Switzerland. Her publications available in English include *A Guide to Child Health* (with Wolfgang Goebel); *A Healing Education*; and *Medicine at the Threshold of a New Consciousness*.

Edmond Schoorel is an anthroposophic physician in Holland who works closely with early childhood teachers to understand human development from pre-birth to age seven. He is author of the book, *The First Seven Years: A Physiology of Childhood*, published by Rudolf Steiner College Press. He currently works in a municipal hospital and has a special interest in early childhood development.

Renate Long-Breipohl taught kindergarten for many years. She now advises and lectures around the world in early-childhood education and with the Sydney (Australia) Rudolf Steiner College. She is the author of *Supporting Self Directed Play in Steiner/Waldorf Early Childhood Education* (WECAN, 2011) and *Under the Stars* (Hawthorn Press, 2012). Her books originate as much from her own experience and research with young children as from Rudolf Steiner, though she believes that engaging with his thinking is a crucial foundation for educators.

Claus-Peter Röh is the leader of the Pedagogical Section of the School of Spiritual Science, based at the Goetheanum, together with his colleague Florian Osswald. Claus-Peter was a class teacher for many years at the Flensburg Waldorf School in northern Germany. He now travels and lectures and consults with Waldorf schools worldwide, and works closely together with IASWECE.

Made in the USA
Charleston, SC
25 September 2012